100 WALKS IN

THE FRENCH PYRENEES

Also by Terry Marsh

The Summits of Snowdonia
The Mountains of Wales
The Lake Mountains: Volumes 1 and 2
The Pennine Mountains

British Library Cataloguing in Publication Data
is available for this title

ISBN 0-340-51517-1

Published by Hodder and Stoughton,
a division of Hodder and Stoughton Ltd,
Mill Road, Dunton Green, Sevenoaks, Kent TN13 2YA
Editorial Office: 47 Bedford Square, London WC1B 3DP

Typeset by Fingertips Publishing Services,
Preston, Lancashire and
SX Composing Ltd, Rayleigh, Essex

Printed in Great Britain by Butler & Tanner,
Frome and London

100 WALKS IN

THE FRENCH PYRENEES

TERRY MARSH

Hodder & Stoughton

LONDON SYDNEY AUCKLAND

FOR GAYNOR

Acknowledgements

Once more my friend Allan Rimmer read part of the manuscript for me, and offered helpful advice for which I am grateful.

But I am especially grateful to Gaynor who accompanied me during the years the book took to prepare and on many of the walks, and transformed into a hardened francophile in the process. Without her support, that of my parents and parents-in-law when it was most needed, I could not have completed the book on time. To them I owe a real debt of gratitude.

CONTENTS

THE 100 WALKS

Section 1: Cirque de Lescun, Vallée d'Aspe – Vallée d'Ossau (west)

6

Section 2: Balaïtous: Ossau (East), Eaux-Bonnes and Val d'Arrens

Section 3: Gave de Labat de Bun to Gave de Gavarnie

Section 4: The Cirques: Gavarnie, Estaube and Troumouse

Section 5: Gave de Gavarnie (East) to Vallée d'Auré

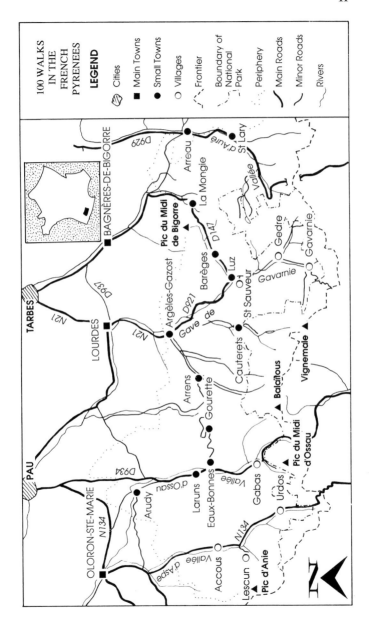

100 WALKS
IN THE
FRENCH
PYRENEES

LEGEND

Cities

■ Main Towns

● Small Towns

○ Villages

Frontier

Boundary of National Park

Periphery

Main Roads

Minor Roads

Rivers

INTRODUCTION

There has long been a popular misconception that the Pyrenees are the preserve of the hardened 'alpinist', that they contain nothing to spark the attentions of regular weekend walkers raised on the comparatively modest heights of Britain and Ireland. At best it is founded on lack of knowledge (which in some measure this book hopes to redress) or an unwillingness among the walking fraternity to forego the undoubted and more widely acclaimed attractions of the Alps for uncertain mountaineering fare further south. At worst it is an arrogant dismissal of one of the finest mountain ranges in Europe.

100 Walks in the French Pyrenees explodes any such notion, offering routes to satisfy walkers of all standards from rugged, high mountain walks based on remote refuges, to serene riverside ambles, from energetic ascents of towering summits to less arduous excursions to mountain lakes and cols. For in the Pyrenees, while there are almost ninety summits that exceed 3000m, most are accessible to every fit walker; hundreds more of lesser height provide virtually limitless opportunity to explore. There are remote, extravagantly wild valleys linked by high mountain passes that will appeal to backpackers, as will the two long-distance trails of the range, the GR10 (Grande Randonnée) and the HRP (Haute Randonnée Pyrénéenne). For lovers of uncomplicated riverside strolls there are countless number, while the botanist and the ornithologist will be in some kind of heaven.

In selecting a hundred walks I have drawn on many years experience among the Pyrenees, and ranged together walks to suit most appetites, grading them so that walkers know what they might expect and to facilitate a progression from the easy to the harder, more demanding undertakings.

Many of the smaller scale maps of Europe represent the Pyrenees as a single chain of mountains forming a natural frontier, a kind of built-in sleeping policeman, between France and Spain, and stretching from the Atlantic to the Mediterranean, a distance of about 400 kilometres (250 miles). Larger maps demonstrate that this is an oversimplification, and that there are really two main ranges, generally, but not always, forming both the watershed and the frontier.

It is terrain of unbelievable contrasts. In France the foothills, rich, verdant, often densely afforested with beech and pine, dissected by cascading rivers and streams that bully their way through narrow valleys, rise abruptly from the plains of Gascony, while in Spain the picture is quite different. On the southern side the scenery is broad, less constricted, far more barren and sun-scorched, with fewer green oases, and the southern limit of the mountains difficult to define because the whole area between them and the great Ebro valley is one of confusing sierras and low, rounded, shadeless hills.

At the western end of the range the land is heavy with moisture borne inland by winds from the Bay of Biscay. Catalonia, to the east, much like the conditions of Spain, is a sweltering region of barren plateaux and valleys draped in lush orchards and vineyards.

The Western range runs from the Atlantic, eastwards to the gap where the Garonne river flows from Spain into France, while the Eastern range, starting some way north of this gap, then runs to the Mediterranean.

North and south of the frontier however lie a number of important massifs. To the north are the Eaux-Bonnes and the Néouvielle group, an alpine landscape of immense grandeur and beauty, with sharp, towering peaks decorated by necklaces of snow and the dying remnants of once immense glaciers. While to the south, entirely in Spain, rise the three highest massifs of the Pyrenees – Perdido, Posets and Maladeta – and an extensive, fragmented range of limestone, at an angle to the frontier, and stretching east-south-east from Le Bisaurin (Sp. Visaurin), close to the frontier just west of the Aragon valley, to Turbon, south of Benasque in the Central Pyrenees. The main summits of this remarkable region are Collarada, Tendeñera and Cotiella, the last of these being the highest in the range.

Running in from the Atlantic, the Pyrenees are no more than gently rolling hills. Here they rise gradually eastwards through the attractive, wooded Basque country for more than 70 kilometres (45 miles) before reaching the true mountains of the Larrau-Haute Soule district, the Pic d'Orhy and Pic d'Anie, the latter being the first of the 2500m+ summits, a delightful introduction to hill walking in the Pyrenees, and the point where this guide begins.

Beyond, further east, lie impressive rock cirques, waterfalls, delicate tarns and lakes that reflect the skys rich blueness, and valleys filled with an immense richness of unique and fascinating flora and fauna.

Along the frontier, between the Pyrénées Atlantiques and the Hautes Pyrénées, heights rise to the 3000m mark, with the magnificent Pic du Midi d'Ossau (2884m: 9462ft) standing in splendid isolation as a challenge not only to ardent rock climbers, but to less intrepid walkers too, especially those with a liking for quality scrambling. Between the valleys of the Aspe and Ossau alone there must be almost a hundred walks well within the capability of anyone reared on the mountains of Wales, the Lake District and the Scottish Highlands.

Further east from Ossau lies a series of frontier peaks and amphitheatres, all over 3000m and separated by high passes – Balaïtous, Vignemale, Le Taillon, the Cirque de Gavarnie. Some of these demand strength and endurance, but almost all can be attained without resort to rock climbing skills or aids, though on a few a rope (and the knowledge to use it) will come in handy. On others, Le Taillon (3144m: 10,315ft), for example, the going is straightforward, but truly spectacular. This is probably the easiest 3000m+ summit in the whole of the Pyrenees, and an exhilarating walk. Still further east, and north, the Pic du Midi de Bigorre (2872m: 9422ft), can virtually be driven up by means of a dusty toll road from the Col du Tourmalet, though there are ascents that avoid these less than acceptable incursions.

A wide sweep is needed to bring you round by the Col d'Aspin to the delights of the vallée d'Aure, the eastern extremity of this guide, and, if you like, the backdoor to the Néouvielle Nature Reserve with its numerous lakes and fine summits.

On an historical note, the whole of the western end of the Pyrenees form the southern boundary of the ancient region of Gascony, regarded by some as England's first empire, for in the Middle Ages English armies occupied this part of France for three hundred years. The Gascons themselves even stood in battle with the English against the French. Gascony embraces six ancient provinces, where you will find the pride of heritage still rumbles on to this day: in the north and bordered on the west by the sea is Landes, while to the east lies Armagnac. Below these two, and spreading themselves along the frontier are the provinces of Basque, Béarn, Bigorre and Comminges. The provinces Béarn and Bigorre roughly equate with the area covered by this book.

Two names are forever linked with the exploration of the Pyrenees, those of Russell and Packe. Count Henry Patrick Marie Russell-Killough (1834-1909), born in Toulouse of a French mother and Irish father, was a romantic eccentric who openly declared himself in love with the Pyrenees, and with Vignemale in particular, while Charles Packe (1826-1896), a Leicestershire landowner was destined to become one of the most influential climbers who in 1862 published his *Guide to the Pyrenees*. Many of the ascents made by Packe and Russell were by routes now considered the *voie normale*, and by comparison with later developments on the great cliffs they fall within the realm of long walks and easy scrambles. More recent exploration concentrated on the cliff faces rather than on the valleys and high corries per se. But inevitably one sport led to another, as the pursuit of newer and more difficult cliff faces started to imprint a network of pathways on the landscape and in the journals and accounts of those who made them. It is these pathways that *100 Walks in the French Pyrenees* now follow.

In 1967 the French authorities designated an irregularly-shaped area in the high Pyrenees, bounded on the south by the frontier, as a national park. It links up with the Ordesa and Monte Perdido national parks on the Spanish side of the frontier. The area covered by the French park is approximately 457 square kilometres. It is totally uninhabited, and its land belongs to the various parishes and communes, not to the park authority. All of the land is at an altitude greater than 1000m (3300ft), and its highest point is Pique Longue on Vignemale at 3298m (10,820ft).

The National Park is surrounded on the French side by a 'periphery', which is treated very much in the same way as the National Park itself. All the walks in this book are contained within either the National Park or the periphery. Prohibitions in the National Park are not dissimilar to those imposed in English and Welsh national parks. Camping is limited to bivouacking in a small tent pitched for the night and struck next morning.

Flora and fauna

The Pyrenees have a greater variety of flora than anywhere else in the mountains of France; local sources put this as high as 570 species, of which some 400 are indigenous.

Even a comparatively simple guide book – *Connaître la Flore des Pyrénées* by Cécile Lemoine and Georges Claustres – lists over 120 species, and is an excellent publication if your French isnt too bad.

The best flower months are June, July and August, and what took my breath away were the blue gentians, whose unmistakable colour leaps at you from the hillsides. I have found *Gentiana kochiana, alpina, verna* and *pyrenaica* without really trying, as well as two of the yellow variety. Even on the highest cols and peaks many plants continue to grow in the brief summer, and it is not unusual to find every crevice or hole in rock faces occupied by flowers. It really is a botanist's paradise, and photographers are well advised to remember to take close up lenses or bellows.

As for fauna, look out for the enchanting izards, the chamois of the Pyrenees, who are slightly smaller than their alpine cousins. There are nearly 4000 in the National Park area, though they are not easy to spot among the rocks: in summer look for them grazing just below the snowline. There are large concentrations in the Ossau Reserve, around Balaïtous and on the high plateau above Gavarnie.

There are about fifty European brown bears still left in the Pyrenees. They live on low forest slopes in the peripheral area, but invariably make off deeper into the forest at the approach of man. Marmots have been introduced from the Alps during the last thirty-five years, and are now well established. Gregarious and inquisitive, they pop up and whistle at you in quite a few places, with the largest concentrations being around Ossau and Néouvielle.

The wild boar can still be found very locally, generally in Spain, but the rarest and most curious of mammals is the desman, a creature a little larger than a rat with a pointed snout and half-webbed feet. It can be spotted along the banks of streams, and outside the Pyrenees is only found in the Caucasus. Ibex, too, once thought to have been shot out of existence, have again been seen, though it is not clear whether they are genuine survivors or individuals that have wandered northwards from other parts of Spain.

The Pyrenees can also boast a richness of birdlife. I once identified more than ninety species over a three-day period, including such niceties as citril finch, red-backed shrike, lammergeyer, snow finch, rock bunting, alpine swift, Egyptian vulture, red kite and a black-throated black-eared wheatear. Alpine accentors are found everywhere, black redstarts constantly grate at you from the cover of rocks, and the cries of alpine choughs echo loudly from the cliff walls.

Though a few golden eagle (about eight pairs) are still to be found in the Pyrenees, any large bird seen circling above you is likely to be a griffon vulture. Its silhouette is quite distinctive, and although there are said to be only about forty-five pairs in the whole range, I counted twenty-seven birds circling high above the Col du Tourmalet in 1987, and have never failed to find them there since.

All these animals and birds are wild and roam free, and under no circumstances must they be disturbed, especially during breeding periods.

Freedom to roam

The people of France seem far less preoccupied than the British over 'rights' of access and, as a rule, walkers in France are free to roam over all open paths and tracks. But the rules of behaviour still apply, and no decent walker will leave gates open, trample crops or damage walls. Smoking or lighting fires is forbidden in forests, and the rule actively enforced. In many of the foothills vineyards and orchards will be encountered; taking fruit from these is simply stealing, and will be treated as such. And in some parts of France there are local laws about taking chestnuts, mushrooms and snails, which are often a local cash crop. Signs like *Réserve de Chasse* and *Chasse Privé* identify land on which the shooting is reserved to the landowner. As in Britain, there is a Country Code, the *Code du Randonneur*. Behave sensibly and you will be tolerated everywhere.

How to get there

The majority of visitors to the Western and Central Pyrenees from Britain will approach from the north. Access both by public and private transport, availability of accommodation, and convenience in terms of minimising time spent reaching a walking destination unite in commending an approach from the French side of the mountains and all these walks are French based.

In Britain, the French Government Tourist Office (178 Piccadilly, London, W1V 0AL: Tel: 071-491-7622. Office hours: Mon-Fri 9am-5pm) offers a massive public information service. Useful publications include *The Traveller in France: Reference Guide* and the *Touring Traveller in France*. They also issue the annual guide to the Logis de France, as well as a host of other useful publications. If writing send a large sae (A4), with not less than £1.00 (1992) in stamps on it.

When in France, the Offices du Tourisme or Syndicats d'Initiative, found in most towns, and certainly in Pau, Tarbes, Oloron-Ste-Marie, Laruns, Gourettes, Argelès-Gazost, Cauterets, Luz-St Sauveur, Gavarnie, La Mongie and St Lary-Soulan, advise on accommodation, restaurants, entertainments, sights and local transport.

If travelling by car the main towns to make for are Pau or Tarbes, from where good roads continue south to penetrate all the valleys mentioned in this guide. By train, it is best to aim for Pau, from where a service still runs to Oloron-Ste-Marie to connect with an SNCF (French railways) bus service down the Aspe valley. The railway line through the valley was cut by a landslide over twenty years ago and remains closed, a forlorn sight. The bus service however still stops at all the abandoned railway stations. Railway-bus services also operate from Buzy into the Ossau valley, to Laruns, Eaux-Bonnes and Gourette, and from Lourdes into the Gave de Pau, to Luz, Cauterets, Barèges and Gavarnie. Other services operate to Tarbes and into the Gave de Gavarnie.

Accommodation

Gîtes d'Etape will be found useful and inexpensive and are best thought of as unmanned youth hostels for people of all ages. They are to be found in many places along the footpath network and are usually signposted. They are quite comfortable, with bunk beds, showers, and well-equipped kitchens. Some have wardens (*guardien*) who may offer meals, but this cannot be relied on. Gîtes d'Etape are intended exclusively for the walker, climber, cyclist, etc., and should not be confused with Gîtes de France which are country cottages available for holiday let.

Camping is officially not permitted in the Pyrenees National Park or the Néouvielle Nature Reserve, but unofficially, if you are more than 1500m from a road, an hours walk from a campsite, or the weather turns bad, and can ask permission if possible, you should not be troubled.

Official camp sites in valleys are generally very good, although the facilities vary from next to nothing to extravagant bars, shops, night clubs, restaurants, and heated swimming pools. *Camping à la ferme* is increasingly popular, more basic than official sites, but perfectly adequate, and allow you to exchange the gentler sounds of farm animals for the late night discos of some official sites.

Mountain huts or refuges The presence or absence of a mountain hut or refuge (*abris*) is unlikely significantly to affect the majority of the walks in this guide. But walkers wanting extended day tours in the mountains, or who do not wish to operate from a valley base will find them invaluable.

Generally, the huts are of an acceptable standard, some are downright luxurious, others (not many) little better than a big, draughty tent. Those of the Club Alpin Français (CAF) usually have keepers, with reduced charges (normally about 50%) for CAF members and members of reciprocating mountaineering clubs, such as the British Mountaineering Council. Huts with keepers provide a meals service (not the cheapest way of eating, but quite generous and substantial), though self-catering is often possible.

The Pyrenees National Park authority has built quite a few attractively located huts aimed rather more at the walker than the climber, and their charges and services are much the same as the CAF.

Full details of all the refuges, huts and shelters, their capacity and facilities are obtainable by writing or telephoning direct to the following addresses.

Organisation	Address	Telephone
Club Alpin Français	Section de Tarbes Résidence Branly 46, Boulevard du Martinet 65000 TARBES	62 36 56 06 (Machine) 62 36 93 23 (Fridays)
Parc National des Pyrénées	59, route de Pau 65000 TARBES	62 93 30 60
Randonnées Pyrénéennes	29, rue Marcel-Lamarque 65000 TARBES	62 93 66 03

Equipment
The equipment required for the walks in this book is little more than might be used on any regular weekend outing to the fells and mountains of Britain. At the very least on all but the easiest

walks this should comprise comfortable mountain boots with Vibram soles, warm socks (two pairs of equal quality help minimise the risk of blisters and chafing), breeches and suitable trousers (wearing shorts is fine providing something warmer is carried in your sac), windproof anorak and waterproofs, hat (preferably wide-brimmed for shade), and gloves, even in summer. A high factor suncream is always a good idea, while a good pair of sunglasses will help reduce eye strain.

Depending on the time of your visit, crampons and ice-axes may prove necessary, but as a rule are not needed during July and August. A rope might come in handy on the Ossoue glacier of Vignemale, or as a psychological aid on one or two of the Grade A walks and a short section of the Pic du Midi d'Ossau, especially if there are young children in the party.

Walkers staying overnight in huts will find a torch (and spare batteries) particularly helpful, and, if you are a light sleeper, some ear plugs! Some form of emergency food that doesnt melt should be tucked away in your sac, along with (more readily to hand) map, compass and whistle.

Campers, backpackers and those intending to make use of mountain refuges will find a sleeping bag that is suitable for British summers more than adequate for use in the Pyrenees. Remember that most of the refuges and high mountain 'wild' campsites are a long way from useful civilisation and cannot be expected to replenish your supplies.

Maps
The maps on which this book is based are the IGN 1:25 000 Série Bleue, Sheets 1547 ouest – Accous; 1547 est – Laruns; 1647 est – Argelès-Gazost/Cauterets; 1648 est – Vignemale; 1747 ouest – Luz-St Sauveur; 1747 est – Campan; 1748 ouest – Gavarnie; 1748 est – Vielle-Aure/St Lary-Soulan.

The newer Top 25 maps, also at 1:25 000, cover much of the same area but not all of the walks in this book and are more expensive, so don't buy them needlessly. IGN also produce a Série Orange at a scale of 1:50 000, not unlike OS Landranger Maps, though they cover a smaller area.

More appropriate for walkers are the 1:50 000 maps produced by Randonnées Pyrénéennes. These are based on IGN maps but are superimposed by paths, pistes, location of refuges, etc., and cover an area of almost 2700 square kilometres, which effectively means you can get away with carrying only two maps, No. 3: Béarn and No. 4: Bigorre, though you may find the reassurance of the larger scale helpful in an area as rugged as the Néouvielle Nature Reserve.

On all the maps, and throughout this book, reference is made to the HRP (Haute Randonnée Pyrénéenne) and the GR10 (Grande Randonnée) – part of a 40,000 kilometres (25,000 miles) network of long distance footpaths in France. These are the two main long distance walks through the Pyrenees, stretching from coast to coast. Of the two the GR10 is the easier, though neither are modest undertakings. The GR10 spends the greater part of its journey on the French side, while the HRP prefers the Spanish side, though both swing about enormously, and occasionally share the same way.

Emergencies

The mountain rescue service in the Pyrenees is impressively efficient and speedy; it is also very expensive and should only be called upon if absolutely necessary.

If an accident does occur in a high or remote part of the range, the first port of call, if possible, should be a manned refuge. Many have radio links with the gendarmerie and can have the rescue service swinging into action in minutes. Whether you head for a refuge or descend to a telephone to call the gendarmerie (dial 17), make sure you carry a map with the position of the injured person clearly marked on it. The map is important, particularly if there are likely to be language difficulties.

Weather

Every mountain area has its own climactic idiosyncrasies, and the Pyrenees are no exception. With the Spanish side baked all day in the sun, and the French side much affected by the prevailing, moisture-laden Atlantic weather systems, it is not unusual, especially in early summer, to trudge to the frontier through drifts of snow or ice and to descend into Spain on barren, bone-dry slopes.

In general, the weather from mid-June to the end of September can usually be relied on to be good, and is rather more predictable than elsewhere in France. During a two-week stay between these dates, more than two or three days spoiled by rain would be a great misfortune.

Temperatures in summer are not as high as the latitude (virtually on a par with Rome) might suggest, but for British visitors they can prove draining, especially in July and August. For this reason it is especially important to start long days very early to maximise the benefit of the cooler mornings, and to make a point of drinking more water than normal.

In the long French valleys, particularly in June and July, thick clouds often appear in the mornings, due to temperature inversion, and remain throughout much of the day, but you can often drive up through them to enjoy your walk beneath clear blue skies and brilliant sunshine. Don't assume that a cloudy day in the valley necessarily means a cloudy day on the tops.

If the day does start bright and clear, there is the possibility of clouds forming in the valleys during the afternoon and rising quickly to the tops, generally to be dispelled during the evening or overnight – another good reason for that early start.

A warm and cloudless day may also breed a sense of false security, and half an hour sheltering from the sudden and often violent storms that appear from nowhere is sure to put you on your guard. These storms usually form south of the watershed as the hot, dry air of Spain meets the cooler airstreams passing from the north. They come with little advance warning, are immensely spectacular (though it was no fun for the young lady I once saw chasing her tent around Lac d'Ayous with lightning spearing the ground all around her!), and pass just as suddenly.

September brings the first of the frosts, and the shepherds down from the mountains as the snow arrives. Quite often, however, September can give truly superb walking days. Likewise October, though now the feel of winter is really in the air, and days of low cloud and rain more frequent.

Winter extends through to March and April, and is not the period for which the walks in this book were intended. Even so, experienced winter walkers will find an incredible and indelible magnificence about the Pyrenees in winter's raiment . . . and twenty million skiers!

Grading of walks

As the Pyrenees offer a range of walks to suit all standards, I have employed a rough grading system, so you will know what you are letting yourself in for. Remember that most walks in the Pyrenees tend to be rather longer than in Britain, and require more time to complete. However, on all trips into the Pyrenees over the three and a half years this book took to prepare, I was accompanied at various stages either by children of nine and ten and parents (then pushing seventy); everyone thoroughly enjoyed themselves and clammered for more. It is hoped you will, too.

Grade A – these routes are suitable only for the experienced (and, preferably, accompanied) mountaineer, accustomed to long and sometimes strenuous days. You can expect to encounter airy traverses and crests, advanced scrambling, routes which are not on paths, some snow and glacier work, overnight stays in refuges, and prolonged exercise at heights usually in excess of 2500m (8000ft).

Grade B – routes in this category are within the capabilities of any regular weekend walker in Britain accustomed to coping with ascents of the Welsh, Lakeland and Scottish mountains (for example). For some routes (eg Le Taillon), ability to use an ice-axe is essential, and a willingness to venture over the 3000m mark (9840ft). In the main, however, this is not the case, though walkers should be prepared for stretches of energetic exercise on most walks. You may find the odd section that has a sense of exposure, a little moderate scrambling (and in the case of the Pic du Midi d'Ossau, quite a lot of moderate scrambling), and the need to cope with short snow slopes. While all walks in the group may be accomplished within one day, there is often advantage in staying overnight in refuges.

Grade C – walks, not necessarily low level, within the capability of every fit person; some uphill work, and not always short walks, but capable of being accomplished safely with hands in pockets (most of the time).

Grade D – simple riverside or lakeside walks requiring no special equipment, but demanding a modest standard of fitness.

Times
The times given for each walk are a calculation combining (a) personal experience both of my own times on the walks and the times of others of varying ages and levels of fitness, (b) times given in French guide books, and (c) on National Park waymarking boards. They are therefore a realistic average; they make no allowances for stops. Where only one time is given it is for the whole walk, which probably doesn't fit into the straightforward up and down variety.

Heights, distances and ascent

Heights are taken from the IGN 1:25 000 Série Bleue maps (see page 22). Conversions to feet are simply metric heights multiplied by 3.2808 and rounded up or down. In the absence of grid references, spot heights are frequently used, though even these vary across different map editions. Heights expressed in the heading to a walk are the highest point achieved on that walk, and may not therefore be the summit of a mountain.

Distances and ascent are seldom used as the nature of the terrain is often a more important factor in the calculation of a walk's duration. Where distances are given kilometres are converted to miles by multiplying by 0.625.

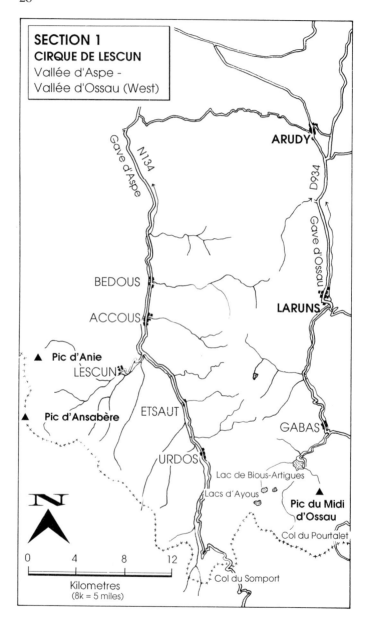

SECTION 1
CIRQUE DE LESCUN
Vallée d'Aspe -
Vallée d'Ossau (West)

SECTION 1: CIRQUE DE LESCUN, VALLÉE DASPE – VALLÉE DOSSAU (WEST)

Walk 1 Pic d'Anie (2504m: 8215ft) Grade B/C Lying to the west of the village of Lescun, Pic d'Anie is the most westerly of the Pyrenean peaks to exceed 2500m. It dominates an extraordinary region that every walker should get to know; a waterless, limestone landscape, in parts almost lunar, and at best quite fantastic, honeycombed and pitted with some of the world's deepest recorded chasms and potholes.

The mountain, the home of wild goats and, according to legend, the source of storms, is claimed by the Basques as their one high Pyrenee, for beyond the boundary marked by its height lies a region of vast forests and old villages, soft pastoral valleys and green moulded hills that tumble benignly to the far off Atlantic Ocean.

Little more than a long walk is needed to conquer Pic d'Anie, and though the views from the summit are extensive the principal heights of the Pyrenees are too far distant to provide any immediate sense of grandeur. Nevertheless, Pic d'Anie is a good introduction to Pyrenean walking, and will serve both to gauge your standard of fitness and endurance and to whet the appetite for more.

1a From Arette la Pierre-Saint-Martin The area between Pierre-Saint-Martin and Pic d'Anie is known as a 'karst' area after a place in the Dinaric Alps in Yugoslavia where the strange limestone formations found here were first investigated. This is not a region to encounter in poor visibility, when Walk 1b from Lescun offers a better chance of success. The frontier along this section of the Pyrenees is ill-defined and not clearly indicated on maps.

Follow the access road heading south through the ski tow area to Pescamou, beneath the frontier summit, Pic d'Arlas, and continue a short distance to some shepherds' huts (Cabanes de Pescamou). Here ascend west over grassy slopes to the obvious Col de Pescamou on the border with Spain (1918m). Cross briefly into Spain and continue southwest then southeast to re-enter France by the Col de Boticotch (1939m). A waymarked (red and yellow stripes) and cairned track continues southeast, through the karst area. For a while the track runs east, through an area of numerous potholes and chasms that could prove disconcerting in mist, before bearing southeast to reach the Col des Anies (2084m), although the word 'col' here loses normal meaning, so chaotic is the terrain. From here head for the minuscule (and often non-existent) Lac d'Anie where the route from Lescun is joined for the final pull to the summit.

Ascent: 3h 30: Descent: 2h 30

1b From Lescun This is the normal French route, an uncomplicated walk with much of interest en route. Only in the

The village of Lescun with Pic d'Anie beyond left.

final stages is the limestone chaos of the karst area encountered. It is a satisfying introduction to walking in the Pyrenees.

From Lescun take the minor road to the Refuge de Labérouat (signposted), and continue past the Refuge on a good track with splendid views of Pic d'Anie, Pic de Countendé, Le Billare and the Anaye valley. The track (part of the GR10) soon enters forest, the Bois du Braca d'Azuns, where it is waymarked (red and white stripes). The forest lies directly beneath some impressive, towering cliffs, Les Orgues de Camplong, though their presence is not noted until you leave the forest.

The track continues uneventfully to a hut, Cabane du Cap de la Baitch (Baigt), which was occupied when last I visited there (in 1989) by a garrulous shepherd, who sells goat's cheese. Near the hut the GR10 heads north over the Pas d'Azuns, but you should follow an ascending track southwest, following the line of a stream which it later crosses and then recrosses as it ascends more steeply to Lac d'Anie, from where you can see your objective ahead and to the left.

Follow the path southwest, away from the Col des Anies into a weird area of limestone hollows and boulders, where the route is cairned, and begin a gentle traverse of the summit's north face, which is a massive slope of scree. The path swings round to the west face before climbing, more steeply, over broken rock to the summit.
Ascent: 3h 30: Descent: 2h 30

Walk 2 Le Billare (2318m: 7605ft) Grade B/C There are actually two peaks here, Le Billare, the higher, and the Petit Billare, but, appearing as one, they present a stunning aspect when viewed from Lescun. The ascent to the main summit is tiring and no more impressive in terms of views than the ascent of Pic d'Anie. But there is a better chance during the summer months

Le Billare from the Lescun valley.

of having the route to yourself.

Begin from the point in the minor road through the Sanchèse hollow where it bends to the southwest, not far from the Maison familiale. Ahead of you rises a needle-like peak, the Pic de la Brèque, beneath which the HRP zigzags up into the broad expanse of the Anaye valley. Follow this route as far as the Anaye huts (1513m), the Cayolars d'Anaye, and from here strike obliquely southwest up the hillside, over grassy slopes to an obvious depression on the long west ridge extending out to the Pics de Pèneblanque; loose boulders and scree are encountered just below the ridge. From the depression it is a fairly easy task to follow the broken ridge to the summit of Le Billare. The highest point is not clear, but there is a strange depression on the summit which might have held a tarn or have been a shallow crater. The view is much the same as from Pic d'Anie.

Ascent: 3h 30: Descent: 2h 30

Walk 3 Lac de Lhurs (1691m: 5548ft) Grade C Hidden high among encircling hills the Lac de Lhurs lies at the end of a fairly energetic ascent into the limestone landscape typical of this splendid region. Out of sight is very much out of mind here, and it would be unusual to encounter anyone save for the odd shepherd. The lake sits comfortably in the bottom of a great bowl of mountains, a sun trap and exceedingly hot during summer months. By contrast the shade of the Bois de Bresme et de Larrangus offers welcome shelter from the heat of midday, as well as providing a wealth of flora and fauna.

Walkers with plenty of time to amble along will find a start from the village of Lescun an easy introduction, leaving by the roadway leading to the Pont de Lauga, and bypassing fields that from July to mid-September are abuzz with haymaking activity as the local farmers prepare winter fodder for their cattle.

Beyond the bridge the road swings to the south to reach spot height 977, just above the Borde d'Anapia, where the road continues southwest (in fact the HRP) along the Gave d'Ansabère. From the spot height, continue however in a northwesterly direction along an unmetalled track that takes you to the foot of the conspicuous cone of Aloun, passing along its southern flank to reach the Larrangus stream. Motorists can drive vehicles to this point, though the track is narrow and the scope for manoeuvre very limited.

Now continue on foot past a ruined farm to a crossroads where an arrow painted on the rocks indicates the route to take. Here we enter the forest, dominated by the towering forms of Le Dec de Lhurs and the commanding Billare. A short stony passage leads into the attractive heart of the forest, mainly beech, many of considerable girth, but interspersed with young conifers.

The track continues to rise until it reaches a wooded crest which overlooks the lower reaches of the Lhurs valley, here known as the Landrosque. Climb with the crest towards the west-northwest taking great care (particularly if there are children in the party) as the track ascends rather sharply in zigzags to pass around a deep ravine at the foot of Le Billare, continuing again with zigzags as you enter the limestone upper section.

On leaving the forest the boulder slopes need care until it is possible to reach and cross the stream issuing from the lake a short distance above. From the lake, surrounded by imposingly high peaks, the great mass of Le Billare and Le Dec de Lhurs command less of our attention than the vertical walls of La Table des Trois Rois. The lake itself in the early part of summer faithfully mirrors the surrounding heights, but as summer progresses its waters subside to leave a sunbaked rim. Return by the outward route.

Time: Round trip: (From Lescun) 6h: (From the Larrangus stream) 4h 30

Walk 4 Pic d'Ansabère (2360m: 7742ft) Grade B On the ascent of the Pic d'Ansabère from the Lescun valley as much pleasure is derived from the approach as from conquering the summit. This is one of a number of towering white limestone summits on the frontier that lie hidden at the head of a side valley, west of the Aspe, and rise high above rich green meadows and forests through which lie all the routes from the French side. Greater attention in this region however has always been given to the two attendants of the Pic, the Aiguilles d'Ansabère. These pinnacles, an imposing sight, are very much the province of the rock climber, and have a reputation for severity earned, as is often the case, at the cost of lives. Some maps of this area are misleading as to the location of the Pic d'Ansabère, which in fact lies *between* the Grande and the Petite Aiguilles; the highest point is the Grande Aiguille (2377m), while the Pic d'Ansabère is some 17m lower.

It has to be said that the final 300m to the summit of the Pic, which is fairly steep and a tumble of scree and boulders, does tempt you to conclude your journey at the Col de Pétragème (Port d'Anso), where the lushness of the French side contrasts with the barren, shadeless desert lying across the frontier in Spain.

The ascent begins from the Pont Lamareich, which is reached from Lescun by a minor road running southwest (part of the HRP), or from further down the valley by turning left at

---

The Aiguilles d'Ansabère and part of the HRP.

The Aiguilles d'Ansabère from the Cabanes d'Ansabère

the Pont du Roy (signposted 'Lhers'), keeping right (for Lescun) after the forest zigzags and later continuing ahead at crossroads. There is ample room to park at the Pont Lamareich, and from here a rough track rises steadily to the Pont Lamary with the white cliffs of Le Dec de Lhurs rising high above the forest, and the famed Aiguilles prominent on the skyline ahead of you. The section between the two bridges is motorable, but not recommended.

Beyond the Pont Lamary the track narrows and ascends through more forest to a large clearing and a ramshackle cabin with a corrugated iron roof. The Aiguilles rise alluringly above all of this delightful section. Little more than an hour (and an enjoyable hour at that) will bring you easily into the heart of this stronghold and lead you to believe that 'it can't be much further'. It can. I once had an extended conversation with a French couple above the Cabanes d'Ansabère which centred on their refusal to believe that the summit still lay a good two hours of hard graft hence, especially hard on a hot day.

From the shepherd's hut cross the stream and regain a prominent path ascending once more into forest. This short section to the Cabanes d'Ansabère is a little tiring, but the massive cirque of peaks which greets you is well worth the effort. The Petite Aiguille is by far the most dominating feature with a sea of scree and boulders rising beneath it to the obvious col (de Pétragème). To the left of the col rises the Pic de Pétragème, followed by an undulating ridge which circles round towards the Pic du Lac de la Chourique, high above a vast grassy hollow through which the HRP wends its way from the Cabanes.

The Cabanes d'Ansabère appear to have been 'modernised' in recent times, and are a group of substantial shepherds' huts, from which, on my last visit, came the sound of snoring to mingle with the ever-present sonic accompaniment of cow bells.

The onward route from the Cabanes may be confusing in mist, because the slightly more prominent HRP path could lead you astray, but your objective is the Col de Pétragème, and in good visibility route-finding should present no problem. The path ascends beneath the Petite Aiguille, and from it you can see how friable these limestone monoliths really are. At the Col, cross into Spain and turn north (right) for the final pull up a tiring slope of scree to a summit that offers a grandstand view of rock climbers' antics on the Grande Aiguille.

Ascent: (From the Pont Lamareich) 4-5 hours: Descent: 2-3 hours

Walk 5 Pic de Laraille (2147m: 7044ft) Grade B/C The ascent of Pic de Laraille is not unduly difficult, but will appeal more to walkers experienced in coping with the rigours of complex and changeable terrain. The route takes you into an area only infrequently visited, and underlines the need for self-sufficiency in an emergency. The competent walker however in search of solitude will be very much at home here.

Begin, as for the ascent of Pic d'Ansabère, at the Pont Lamareich, though there is rather more justification, given the nature of the route, for driving to the Pont Lamary.

A short distance before Pont Lamary a path, unclear in places, heads south-southwest through meadows, and finally enters forest as you approach the Riou de Lazerque. Continue through the forest, always on the true right bank of the valley, until the track reaches a clearing littered with large boulders, and from here move obliquely west until you reach the Cabane Bourrégué.

From the hut the path continues southwest, and later south, until it loses itself in a large grassy and rocky couloir which leads finally to the Col de Laraille.

At the Col you need to cross into Spain for a while, but in the main you should follow the frontier ridge, negotiating en route a rocky pinnacle, beyond which the ridge continues uneventfully to the summit.

Ascent: (From Pont Lamareich) 3h 30-4h: Descent: 2h 30-3h
Ascent: (From Pont Lamary) 3h-3h 30: Descent: 2h-2h 30

Walk 6 Col de Pau (1942m: 6371ft) Grade C, Pic Cotdugoy (2019m: 6624ft) Grade B/C, and Pic Lariste (2168m: 7113ft) Grade B A splendid trio of possibilities, this excursion is decidedly off the beaten track, yet remains an attraction for many inquisitive summer visitors. All three points, and an intermediate top, Marmida (2076m), lie on the frontier, and the walk proves to be a good introduction to walking in the Pyrenees.

The key to the ascent is the long and narrow valley of the Labrénère, due south of the village of Lescun. All the roads into this remarkable side valley have serpentine qualities, so it does not matter by which route you enter Labrénère. A motorable road (Be warned: the French – *'Une route carrossable'* – is often a sweeping generalisation for tracks, tarred and untarred, that range from genuinely motorable highways to something that would put a tank out of action!) heads into the valley and ends at spot height 1112, where there is room to park what is left of your car. (Don't worry, this one isn't too bad, though it is narrow in places and twists about a lot). At the end of the road cross to the true right bank of the stream where a good path leads southwards to the Pont d'Itchaxe (1360m) from where it ascends in zigzags to the Cabanes d'Itchaxe and du Pénot.

From the cabanes the path, still well marked, continues west by more zigzags and then heads generally south to the Col de Pau and a glimpse into Spain.

Ascent: 2h 30: Descent: 1h 30

Two peaks dominate the Col; to the southeast, Pic de Burcq and to the north, Pic Cotdugoy, rather more of a large hillock than a daunting mountain prospect, but all these frontier summits require care and attention, and should not be underestimated. Even so, the easy slopes of the Spanish side will soon whisk you to the summit for a delightful view along the frontier ridge, over Marmida to Pic Lariste.

Marmida offers little resistance, and is followed by a short descent to a shallow col (2019m) from where wide slopes, a little steeper than anywhere else along this stretch of the frontier, lead to the summit; a small gap and a steep pinnacle are passed (keep them on your right) just before the summit.

Ascent and Descent: 1h from Col de Pau

Experienced walkers will find a rugged descent from the col (2019m), rather north of east, to the ascending path not over-demanding. Less experienced walkers should opt for the easier (and frankly more pleasing) retreat by the outward route.

Walk 7 Pic de Burcq (2105m: 6906ft) Grade B/C Strong walkers could easily add Pic de Burcq to the route (Walk 6) over Pic Cotdoguy and Pic Lariste, scampering up and down from the Col de Pau in little more than an hour.

A shorter day awaits walkers content with just the one summit on their day's itinerary, a summit however with a rather more open view than that afforded by Walk 6, and one on which it is very tempting to rest awhile, comfortably ensconced against the breezes that rise up from the hotlands of Spain.

Follow Walk 6 as far as the Col de Pau, from where a direct ascent either on the Spanish side or the French side of the ridge may comfortably be made. The normal route however loops out from the ridge, east and then south, on the French side, before returning to the frontier south of the summit, at the Col de Burcq (2063m). Fifteen minutes is all that should be needed then to follow the summit ridge north to the highest point.
Ascent: (From Col de Pau) 0h 30-1h according to route
Descent: (To Col de Pau) 0h 30

Walk 8 Pic de Labigouer (2175m: 7136ft) A splendid and easily-ascended summit with a vast panorama, the Pic de Labigouer is the highest point along a fine ridge sandwiched between the valleys of Labadie and Belonce. The area is generally well populated with marmots and izards, and overflown by a wide range of buzzards, eagles and vultures; ptarmigan, too, frequent the higher slopes.

8a By the Col de Barrancq Grade B/C The Col de Barrancq is the weakness chosen by the GR10 to slip across the mountains to Borce in the main Aspe valley, and it serves equally well to begin an ascent of Pic de Labigouer.

From the hamlet of Lhers either travel south along the road

to a junction (near spot height 997) where the GR10 ascends through meadows as far as a new forest track which goes down (north) to Lhers, or follow this track from Lhers to the same point. The steep hillside is tackled in zigzags, alternately walking through woodland or across open spaces ripe in summer with bilberries, and in spite of the uphill work has a relaxing air about it. The retrospective view across the Lescun amphitheatre, the distant village itself clinging tenaciously to the hillside, is quite breathtaking.

Back in the forest it is important to follow carefully the GR10 waymarking, especially as much of the way is accompanied by a track servicing a television relay station on a minor outlying top, Le Tuquet. As this track swings north take care to press on upwards to finish with a final steep flourish at the Col de Barrancq.

Having now gained the crest of the ridge follow it right (west of south) until, in a few hundred metres, the forest is left behind and a superb view opens up of the Aspe valley, the great Sesques massif to the east, and, in the far distance, southeast, the Pic du Midi d'Ossau. Ahead now lies the long undulating ridge to the Pic de Labigouer, an exhilarating undertaking with long, sweeping drops on either side that need hold no fear for anyone in clear summer conditions.

More immediate is the minor top (1913m) at the northern end of a short level ridge. A steepish pull is needed from the edge of the forest, and some of the ascent may be eased by traversing across the eastern flank of the hill to the Col de la Nabe (1849m), followed by a more gentle ascent to the top. A more or less level stretch of ridge comes next, followed by a short descent to the Col des Pisés, from where the northern top of Pic de Labigouer holds the promise of more sweat and toil, but this, too, may be turned by contouring due south from the Col des Pisés to reach the eastern ridge, from where the Col de Labigouer is easily gained. Strong walkers however are unlikely to let a mere height saving of 25m deflect them from the true crest of the ridge.

From the Col de Labigouer an easy ridge runs up to the summit and its magnificent panorama.

Ascent: (From Lhers) 3h 30: Descent: 2h 30

8b By the Col de Souperret Grade B The key to this ascent is the route to the Cabane det Caillau (1507m) at the head of the Labadie valley. Access, however, is restricted during summer months, and though vehicles may sometimes be taken as far as the parking area near the Cabane de Pourcibo, it is more likely that you will encounter a closed barrier at the entrance to the National Park, near Aumet, and this inevitably will add time to the day. Without the addition of a walk from Aumet, the route is significantly shorter than that via the Col de Barrancq, and rather more strenuous; strong and experienced walkers will therefore find it an entertaining possible diversion on an off day.

The Cabane det Caillau is a good shelter, if needed, but it is occupied by shepherds during the summer pasturage, and that often means protracted, but friendly, conversations about anything and everything if you come within hailing distance: not the place to practise one's French however, the local dialect is all but unintelligible to most British (and for that matter many French) ears.

From Aumet a stony track continues to the Cabane de Pourcibo and on to the Cabane det Caillau from where a National Park footpath (waymarked) begins its journey southeast through rising meadows to climb to the Col de Saoubathou. After about half a kilometre this path branches. Follow the left fork (northeast) which climbs a rock barrier and then in zigzags to the Col de Souperret. A fine ridge leaves the Col, heading north and then northeast to the summit cairn; there is no path along this section and a few short rocky

problems to negotiate, but the going is nowhere difficult.
Return by the outward route.
Ascent: (From Aumet) 3h: Descent: 2h 30

An alternative, longer, and more interesting descent may be made from the Col de Souperret, and is well worth adding if there is time. From the Col a waymarked path heads southeast, contouring round Table de Souperret to the Col de Saoubathou on a more or less level path. The view across the Bois de Belonce is quite attractive, and the region around the Cabanes d'Ibosque, nestling in a high corrie, is inhabited by marmots.

At the Col de Saoubathou the National Park footpath (waymarked) is regained and followed throughout its many twists and turns back to the Labadie valley. (Add about two hours for this extension).

Walk 9 Lac and Refuge d'Arlet (2020m: 6627ft) Grade C High in its grade, this fine mountain circuit shows something of the way of life of Pyrenean shepherds and offers a vast range of flora and fauna. The walk is on well-defined footpaths, the upper section shared with the HRP: not at all over-demanding, but nor is it a leisurely stroll if the full tour is undertaken.

The starting point is an isolated farm, Terrailh, high in the side valley of Baralet, west of Urdos. The key turning is at the Pont d'Urdos, just south of the Fort du Portalet, where a narrow, winding road works its way to the tiny hamlet of Aubise. Follow the road as it rises steeply in sweeping zigzags for what seems like an eternity, but in reality only a little over four kilometres. Some maps show a parking area at 1210m, but it is better (if the full circuit is intended) to park near Terrailh farm. Most of the surrounding mountain pastures are used to grow winter crops for cattle and sheep, and little thought is needed to recognise that on these steep and remote hillsides haymaking is very much a labour-intensive business, the terrain being far too steep for machines.

Continue from the farm along the road until finally you enter the National Park. Near the Cabane Pacheu a footbridge takes the path across the stream. Gradually, the path, always broken and stony climbs steeply in zigzags to the headwall of the valley, known as the Montagne de Banasse. In reality, it is the Pics d'Arri, d'Arlet and d'Aillary which form the mountain, while 'Banasse' is simply a high mountain pasturage shared by the communes of Bedous and Accous. Many of these communal pasturages have unusual rules of tenure, relics of ancient disputes and wranglings between shepherds struggling to eke an existence for their flocks from the roughest of environments. In this case the pasturage belongs for four years to one commune, and only for the fifth to the other. Similar 'nonsensical' arrangements exist in numerous locations along the frontier, while elsewhere the conditions of pasturage are well documented and rigorously observed.

As you climb towards the headwall you pass a number of shepherds' huts. On fine days it is all too easy to romanticise and think how wonderful their life must be. But the reality is a solitary existence from June to September, at least two hours from the nearest road and a long way from home and family, spent tending flocks and making cheese which for many of them is not only their only source of income, but the mainstay of their diet, too. Throw in days when the mists never clear, when rain persists hour after hour, and electrical storms crash about the mountainsides with a vengeance, and suddenly some of the romance flakes away. Small wonder visitors are often seized upon for news of the rest of the world!

After a while the National Park path meets the HRP near the ancient Cabane des Caillaous, where a troupe of marmots have taken up residence.

Shortly, the path crests a small hilltop and reaches its greatest elevation just east of Lac d'Arlet, from where Pic d'Anie can be seen to dominate the Cirque de Lescun to the northwest just as the Pic du Midi d'Ossau holds the eye to the east. Nearby, the Refuge d'Arlet, a National Park hut with guardian (from 1 July – 15 September), is a justly popular place.

From the hut descend northwest in zigzags until at a waymarked junction you pick up the National Park path leading into the Belonce valley. The Bois de Belonce is a scrappy affair in places, comprising more undergrowth than the fine stands of beech and conifers found lower down. This is especially true near the Cabane d'Hortassy, but a swift flight of zigzags soon has you back in meadowland, strolling along a gradual descent into the valley until on the boundary of the National Park a signpost indicates the route to Col de Lagréou. Follow the path leading to the Col, re-entering forest and facing you with quite a stiff pull at the end of a long day. Eventually, you achieve the Col and can pick out the Terrailh farm far below. A few more sweeping zigzags return you to the starting point by the farm.

Time: 8h

Walk 10 Lac d'Estaëns (Ibon de Astanès) (1775m: 5823ft) Grade C This walk, high in its grade, leads into countryside much used in summer for the grazing of sheep and cattle, a feature that characterises much of the high Aspe valley. Lac d'Estaëns lies across the frontier in Spain, where it is known by the name, Ibon de Astanès, though more than half of the walk remains within the Pyrenees National Park and uses the HRP.

The walk begins from a parking area at Sansanet, about two kilometres south of Forges d'Abel along the N134. Just before the Sansanet hairpin a rough road descends obliquely right to the parking area.

From the parking area locate a broad track descending to a bridge across the infant Gave d'Aspe. Follow the path round to a meeting of pathways, and continue ahead, shortly climbing in zigzags through the woods (mainly beech) to a clearing where the path forks and the Cabane d'Escouret can be seen a short distance ahead.

Before reaching the Cabane fork left and climb fairly easily across mountain grassland to the frontier (marked by a post), and continue west to a grassy saddle which brings Lac d'Estaëns into view directly ahead.

From the saddle a path, as much used by sheep and cattle as by human interlopers, descends to the lake, which on a calm day mirrors the surrounding peaks. According to legend, the lake we see today was once a beautiful meadow from which the cattle came down in autumn, their coats thick and luxurious. One day Saint Jean came on a pilgrimage seeking hospitality, but it coincided with a day when the shepherds were gathering for a celebration, and the saint was turned away. The next day the pasture was transformed, and the shepherds and their sheep drowned in a lake that had suddenly appeared. Tradition has it that the visitor was our Lord, and the shepherds were being punished for their inhospitality. The place is also said to be haunted by the Devil in the form of a black ram, evidence of whose presence comes every spring when black lambs are born to white ewes.

The path runs north not far from the lake, while to the northeast the wine-coloured rocks, sandstone and schist of Pic de Gabedaille (also known as the Signal d'Espélunguère) catch the eye as the path regains the frontier at the Port de Bernère (Pas de l'Echelle).

Just across the frontier the significance of the Pas de l'Echelle is realised, for here the descent is by way of a metal ladder for a short distance, and demands a little care. The onward route now descends quickly to regain the forest, where the path is particularly well adorned by wild flowers that have a liking for limestone.

On leaving the forest the path reaches the pastures of

Espélunguère, where it starts heading east almost horizontally. Soon the path re-enters the forest and continues uneventfully to the Cabane d'Escouret, famous for its cheese, and from which the outward route is soon rejoined.

Time: 5h

Walk 11 Pas d'Aspe (1675m: 5495ft) Grade C The Pas d'Aspe is a narrow, steep-sided and boulder-filled gorge in which the river, descending rapidly from the frontier, forms a number of impressive cascades. It is a route by which a number of the summits of the Aspe, all of them in Spain, may be reached, but it is not easy and should be left to walkers experienced at scrambling, for whom a path ascends from the parking area at Sansanet (signposted). A better (and safer) approach is from a little higher towards the Col du Somport, at Peyrenère.

The walk begins from a bridge at point 1405 along the N134, with popular winter holiday centres above and below the road. There is usually room to park cars nearby, and to the south the Aspe group is clearly seen.

Initially the path is rather vague, but cairned, and leaves the road just below the bridge to head south along a grassy crest towards a wood. Once in the wood the path is more evident, broad and clear (HRP), and leaves it after about one kilometre to climb easily, crossing the Causiat stream (1549m), over mountain pasture to a rough cirque with a steep cliff rising to the right.

The path forks at this point, the left track making more directly for Pic d'Aspe, while the right path traverses below the cliff on scree and boulders to the frontier at the Pas d'Aspe.

Ascent: 1h 30: Descent: 1h

Walk 12 Col d'Iseye (1829m: 6000ft) Grade C Walk 18 describes an ascent to the Col d'Iseye from the vallée d'Ossau, and the two routes combined make an excellent traverse of the range between the Aspe and the Ossau valleys. The present walk confines itself to the ascent from the vallée d'Aspe, one of the finest walks from the valley, and one that quickly rises from the great plain of Bedous into the heart of the mountains, more than rewarding the effort of getting there. This is quite a long walk, even from the end of the approach road, with almost 1000m of ascent.

From Accous, once the capital of the semi-autonomous Aspe valley, a minor road climbs beside the church; though quite narrow the road, formerly a cart track, is now motorable and continues well into the mountains. Not long after leaving the village ignore a road climbing left, and continue across the Pont de Chaguyre, from where the road continues between stone walls and hedgerows, through meadows, small copses and passing numerous barns. Further on another minor track goes left, the Route Forestière de Bergout, and shortly after this it is possible to park a few cars near the Araillé stream (850m).

Now on foot, cross the stream (often dry in summer) and take the path above and parallel to the stream bed (waymarked in red and yellow by the Association Départemental des Sentiers d'Excursions). The path is quite wide and climbs easily through undergrowth to mountain pastures not far from the Cabane du Lapassa and immediately below the cliffs of Ronglet, Montagne de Liard. Directly east the Col d'Iseye has been beckoning for a while, reached now by a never-ending series of short zigzags, and passing en route the Cabane d'Escurets, like the Cabane du Lapassa, occupied during the summer months, and renowned for their incumbents' cheese-making. When the Escurets hut is reached turn right and climb over grass to the col.

Beyond the col the waymarked path continues down into the vallée d'Ossau.

Ascent: 3h: Descent: 2h 15

Walk 13 L'Escarpu (Pic de Sesques) (2606m: 8550ft) Grade B A long and tiring route with more than 2000m (6500ft) of ascent, far from shelter and suitable only for strong walkers who want to get away from it all.

Leave the village of Etsaut between the church (left) and the Post Office and ascend by an alleyway which soon degenerates into a path. The path is steep, but in good condition and climbs along the right bank of the Sadum stream. Higher up, as the path enters undergrowth it becomes less obvious, but then waymarks on rock start to appear as the valley narrows. Near point 962 a stream joins from the northeast, the Ruisseau d'Ourtasse, and you should follow the right bank of this rather steeply through woodland to a couloir falling from Pic d'Aygarry, which zigzags until the path finally leaves the wood for high mountain pasture.

Now cross obliquely to the south to gain the right bank of the Yèse stream, and in a short distance locate the Cabane de Yèse behind a small outcrop.

From the cabin (occupied during summer) climb again on the right bank of the stream, later crossing it and heading north towards a col (2256m). Once on the col head east up a high bouldery corrie to gain the northwest ridge of the mountain, by means of which the final easy pull to the top may be achieved. Ascent: 3h 30-4h: Descent: 2h 30-3h

Walk 14 Chemin de la Mâture (800m: 2625ft) Grade C/D The Chemin de la Mâture is a wondrous creation, a great slicing incursion into vertical limestone cliffs, as if some giant of old has hacked at it with a sword. Opened in 1772, this man-made passage across sheer rock walls was used for transporting tree trunks from the forest above to become masts in Louis XIVs expanding navy.

The way overlooks the narrow Hell's Gorge, through which

Chemin de la Mâture. This ancient way was originally constructed to move timber for ships' masts.

thunders the Sescoué river. Its crossing is quite an experience, and though steep drops are but a stride away, the path is quite wide and need worry no one. Of particular note is the amazing variety of wild flowers that benefit from the sheltered environment, colonising the limestone cliffs in what is a rather grey and otherwise dismal stretch of countryside.

The Chemin is easily tackled from the Pont de Cebers, south of Etsaut on the N134 through the Aspe valley. Here a minor road leaves the N134 by the bridge, where there is a National Park signboard and room to park a few cars. It rises easily above the valley and in a short while, at a tight bend, there is another parking place. The Chemin de la Mâture can be said to begin from here.

Follow a stony path for about half a kilometre, bringing the ancient Fort du Portalet into view, originally a resort for political prisoners, but used as recently as the last war.

On reaching this point the path turns a corner and suddenly the Chemin de la Mâture awaits, a gently rising track, like a tunnel with half its side missing. Above and below rock climbers find endless entertainment, and on a warm summer's day, sheltered from prevailing winds, a picnic high above the gorge watching the games climbers play is very much the change that is as good as a rest.

By continuing along the Chemin a small clearing, Perry, is reached, and walkers doing no more than inspect the Chemin should return from here, taking little more than one and a half hours for the return trip. The path, in fact the GR10, continues much further, of course, turning southeast and leaving the woods for the open vallée de la Baigt de Saint Cours (Sencours), by means of which it is possible to traverse into the upper reaches of the Ossau valley.

Time: 1h 30

Walk 15 Peyrenère to Urdos via Refuge de Larry (1840m: 6037ft)
Grade C For the unadulterated satisfaction of wandering for the sheer pleasure it brings there can be few better excursions than the Tour de la Haute Vallée d'Aspe. It is a monumental trog around the upper part of the valley, much of which has already been encountered on Walk 8 (Pic de Labigouer), Walk 9 (Lac and Refuge d'Arlet), and Walk 10 (Lac d'Estaëns). Not by chance does it share the route in common with the HRP, and that alone says much about the nature of the walk.

The present walk merely continues this tour on the eastern side of the Aspe valley, starting just below Col du Somport, at Peyrenère, and ending in Urdos. It is a long walk, high in its grade, and demands a good standard of fitness and awareness of the mountain environment, but the scenery is magnificent and acutely revitalising.

From the bend just above the Chalet Cadier a path (signposted 'Refuge de Larry') launches itself northwards, climbing easily across the lower slopes of Pic d'Arnousse, and continuing around the lower Pic d'Arnoussère where it bends east and southeast to drop into the Arnousse valley.

Just below the Cabane d'Arnousse, cross the stream by a footbridge and climb through woodland to cross the Gouetsoule stream, taking the sting out of some of the ensuing ascent by wide zigzags until the Col de Gouetsoule is reached. A gradual descent over about one kilometre follows to the Refuge de Larry.

From the refuge descend northwest, steeply at first and entering woodland for a while, and later crossing a stream near the Cabane de Sauquet, just above the Pont de Coustey. It is feasible to make a direct descent to the valley from the bridge, following the stream, but the main route, rather more difficult to follow coming up than going down, heads northwest to the edge of the Bois de Lagaude, before turning abruptly to retreat south and then north again to the farm at Claverie-Saou.

From the farm descend through woodland again to reach Urdos opposite the customs post. (Note: It is unlikely that you will be asked for your passport, but have it with you, just in case. Generally, bona fide walkers are permitted to wander back and forth across the frontier without hindrance, but even customs officials have off days!)
Time: 4h 30-5h

Walk 16 Urdos to Lac de Bious-Artigues via Refuge de Larry and Col d'Ayous (2201m: 7221ft) Grade B/C This and the following walk are but two of a number of long and entertaining links between the Aspe and Ossau valleys; strong and experienced walkers could probably invent more. They are generally more useful to walkers wanting to make long traverses, stopping overnight in refuges, and moving on the next day. But if transport difficulties can be resolved the crossing will provide an intimate acquaintance with some of the finest mountain wandering the Pyrenees have to offer.

Directly opposite the customs post in Urdos (784m) a path climbs steeply away from the road, changing direction a few times before settling for a southerly course across meadows. As soon as the farm at Claverie-Saou is reached however the path makes a great sweeping curve northwards, only to change its mind after half a kilometre and return to a southeasterly direction. With little to trouble fit walkers, the path continues climbing to a small plateau and the Refuge de Larry.

From the Refuge follow the National Park path, across the Hourquette de Larry and on to Col d'Ayous. (Note: The Hourquette de Larry is not named on maps, and should not be confused with the Col de la Hourquette de Larry (2055m), half a kilometre to the northwest.)

At the Col d'Ayous the immense form of Pic du Midi d'Ossau looms into view, while below lie the Refuge d'Ayous and the Ayous lakes. A good path descends easily to the north of Lac Gentau, then passing north of two more lakes before turning northeast and descending into woodland as it makes for the northern end of the Plaine de Bious, from where a wide path leads down to Lac de Bious-Artigues.
Time: 5h-6h

Walk 17 Peyrenère to Lac de Bious-Artigues via Refuge de Larry and Col d'Ayous (2201m: 7221ft) Grade B/C Another excellent link between the Aspe and Ossau valleys, rather longer than Walk 16, and best reserved for a bright clear day when walkers with a similar disposition to the author may experience a great reluctance to return to the valley much before sunset (in which case remember to take a torch!).

Little additional description is justified here: follow Walk 15 as far as the Refuge de Larry, and Walk 16 from there to Lac de Bious-Artigues.
Time: 6h+

Walk 18 Lac d'Isabe (1925m: 6315ft) and Col d'Iseye (1829m: 6000ft) Grade C The great beech and pine cloak of the Bois d'Arrioucau and its companions, the Bois du Bitet and Bois de Sesques, through which this walk goes, are worked intensively. Normally this presents few problems, but when they do occur it is in the form of a closed access road or *camions* lumbering towards you on a narrow road with few opportunities to pass. Neither of these make life uncomfortable for walkers *à pied,* but anyone wanting to shorten the day by driving part of the way runs the risk of a close encounter of the log-laden lorry kind.

The access road, when it is open, extends as far as the Prise d'Eau du Bitet (1150m) some 400m (1300ft) of ascent above the Ossau valley, and reason enough for chancing it; the walk in to the same point is almost 4 kilometres (2.5 miles), and keeps to the right bank of the Gorges du Bitet, either on the access road or by forest trails, until forced across the river a short way west of the Cabane de Raziès.

The Route Forestière du Bitet leaves the D934 400m above the Miégebat hydro-electric station, and room to park a few cars can be found on both sides of the road nearby.

Lac d'Isabe: the Lac d'Isabe lies high in a glacial corrie that retains snow and ice well into summer, and this can have the effect of raising the grade of this walk from an already high C to B. Nevertheless, its setting is most attractive and the lake rarely visited outside the main holiday month of August.

From the end of the *route forestière* ford the Iseye stream and pass through a fine plantation of beech trees. The start is a little steep, and the route waymarked (blue flash on white background). For a while the angle eases, but not for long as the path climbs even more steeply and then in zigzags. Along this stretch, by way of taking your mind off aching legs, notice how the nature of the forest is changing; the trees now are not so fine, smaller and more twisted, the trunks are bent from the base due to the pressure of snow, while higher up on the limits of the forest the trees show evident signs of avalanche damage.

On leaving the forest you enter a region of boulders and scree where the path is less obvious. To the right the Cascades d'Isabe are a notable sight, as is the twisted and variable strata of the surrounding peaks and rock walls, a great geological mishmash of metamorphic rocks (about 350 million years old) overlaid by more recent limestone rocks (65-100 million years), and the whole lot distorted like child's plasticine by the great earth movements that brought what is now Spain crashing into the immoveable central massif to the north.

The path now continues into a sort of small valley that is left by crossing a small rocky outcrop on the right. The terrain is a mass of blocks and boulders and necessitates a lot of to-ing and fro-ing until the path finally and quite unexpectedly leads to the lake, only discovered at the last moment.

Time (From Miégebat): 3h 30

Col d'Iseye: from the end of the road follow the path ahead, across a ditch and climb quickly through the forest, now cleared in many places, and leading to pastures near the Cabane de Cujalate. Keep the Cabane on the left and continue ahead to re-enter the forest which in places is starting to recolonise the clearings. Just after a stream joins from the left, you need to cross the valley stream, here the Colcharas. Oddly, although still some way from the Col d'Iseye, an obvious boundary between the Aspe and Ossau valleys, the actual demarcation line occurs just below the confluence of these two streams, where you pass from the canton of Laruns to that of Accous. Local history puts forward two reasons for this; one that the loss of the Ossau side of the valley to Accous was as a result of a jumping contest held during a local fête, the other that it resulted from the repayment of debt.

Pic Peyreget and part of La Grande Raillère de Pombie.

Continue climbing steeply through the forest, noting the yew trees that have started to appear. On leaving the forest you reach the Plaine de Characou, which in summer is decked with the two species of yellow gentian, *lutea* and *burseri*, the latter distinguished by its paler yellow flowers touched with brown.

For a while the path follows the upper limit of the forest, and then crosses the stream issuing from a ravine to climb to the Cabane Laiterine just below the Col d'Iseye, now only a short distance away.

Time (From Miégebat): 3h 30

Walk 19 Pic du Midi d'Ossau (2884m: 9462ft) Grade B By Pyrenean standards Pic du Midi d'Ossau is of modest elevation, yet its unique profile, and the bold way it dominates the landscape, give it a grandeur greater than higher mountains elsewhere in the range, and have earned it considerable respect since the first recorded attempt to climb it in 1552 by François de Foix – and even his account of the ascent makes reference to someone having been there before. The mountain stands apart from others in the range, rather like the Matterhorn, and those few peaks that are close by are lower and comparatively insignificant. In many ways the symbol of the Pyrenees, it is indeed a mountain of classic proportions, rising from green meadows dressed in spring with a splendid variety of flowers, its stark, granite walls calling every walker in the Pyrenees sooner or later as surely as the church bell calls the faithful to worship. Rock climbers know it well, and there are probably more routes

A good path leads from the Col de Suzon to the foot of the superb scramble to the summit of Pic du Midi d'Ossau.

on the walls of 'Jean-Pierre', as it is affectionately known, than on any other Pyrenean mountain.

Less gymnastic mortals however need not fear that Jean-Pierre is barred to them, for there is a fine extended scramble capable of being tackled by walkers of almost any age. Young children and those with some sensitivity to heights will however find comfort in the security of a rope from time to time, although for most this is unnecessary in normal conditions. The key to the walkers' ascent is the Col de Suzon, which lies between the Pic du Midi d'Ossau and a minor acolyte, Pic Saoubiste, on a broad grassy ridge. There are a number of ways of reaching the Col de Suzon, and these are described in Walk 20 (the Tour of Pic du Midi d'Ossau). The shortest, and one which springs Jean-Pierre dramatically into view as you crest an intervening ridge, starts a short distance north of the Col du Pourtalet, at a car parking area known as Anéou; the whole of this final upper section of the Ossau valley is open and spacious, and the car park easily located.

From the car park cross a stream by a wooden bridge and follow an obvious path, past a shepherds hut (Cabane de Sénescau), rising, in due course in zigzags, to the summit of a broad grassy ridge, which is crossed at the Col du Soum. This is the point where the full impact of Pic du Midi d'Ossau hits you, and a splendid place to rest for a while after the exertions of the ascent so far. Ahead, directly beneath the mountain you will see the Refuge de Pombie, and this is easily reached by a descending path.

Just before the Refuge a second path goes left towards the Col de Peyreget, but you should continue ahead to skirt a tarn, the Lac de Pombie, and reach the Refuge.

Beyond the Refuge you enter a region known as La Grande Raillère de Pombie, which has to be the mother and father of all rock falls, the full extent of which is not so obvious at close hand. Follow the path, such as it is, through this ankle-twisting terrain, which brings you directly beneath the Pombie wall of Jean-Pierre, and continue in due course on a rising path to the Col de Suzon where you cross into the pastoral loveliness of the Magnabaigt valley with its herds of ponies and small groups of izard, the Pyrenean chamois.

It may not seem it, but from the Col it will take good walkers up to two and a half hours to reach the summit of Pic du Midi, with at least another one and a half to two hours for the return. If you do not have the time, the energy or the inclination I suggest that you opt instead for a short excursion to the nearby Pic Saoubiste. It isn't the difficulty which consumes the time, but the fact that you are embarking on an extended and exhilarating scramble on which care and concentration are essential.

The initial approach to the foot of the scramble (2345m) is a

Retrospective from the ascent of Pic du Midi d'Ossau to the Col de Suzon and the Balaïtous massif beyond.

rising grassy ridge, crested with rock outcrops, but which present no difficulty. The first problem is a chimney, in which there used to be iron stanchions, but these have now been removed; there are however many good holds, and the chimney is not difficult. At the top move left up a short sloping slab with a moveable peg which can be placed in one of several holes to ease your progress, but take care over the positioning so that you do not cause problems for yourself or others on the descent.

An obvious path (occasional cairns) then turns right across the face to the foot of a second, open chimney, with a broken slab to its right (which for some may prove easier than the chimney). The chimney has good holds, but is a little longer than the first; there is an iron peg near the top, on the right. It is important to realise that from this point on there is a significant risk of stonefall if there is a party ahead of you.

At the top of this chimney the path continues to rise across the face, almost reaching the North face of the mountain, but a cairn a short distance from it (about 35m) marks the entrance (left) to a gully of easy rock which leads to a long sloping groove (sometimes described as a third chimney). A few pegs are still in place here, but they are not needed. However, at the top of this groove note an iron post with a pointed indicator (2657m); this marks the start of the route in descent, and an essential location if poor visibility is encountered.

The route now continues over the wide roof of the mountain, a gentle slope known as the Rein de Pombie, which is an agonising moonscape of broken rocks and scree, crossed by numerous paths. From the head of the groove bear half left until the edge of the South cirque is reached, which you should follow to the first summit, Pointe de France (2878m). This is not the highest point; the true summit, Pointe d'Espagne (2884m) is about 100m distant and reached by a very narrow ridge, incised on both sides by steep gullies, and calling for care.

After all the effort the summit is rather flat and uninteresting, but the view, as might be expected, is magnificent, especially to the east; across the Ossau valley is seen the val d'Arious with the fine pyramid of Pic Palas at its head, and, right, the massive form of Balaïtous, and, beyond that, more distant, Vignemale. Ascent: 4h 30-5h: Descent: 3-4h.

Walk 20 Tour of Pic du Midi d'Ossau (2208m: 7244ft) Grade B/C Unquestionably, this route is one of the finest walking circuits in the whole of the Pyrenees, offering a landscape at once rugged and pastoral, the grand mountain standing high above its pastures and meadows where izards and wild goats roam and marmots fuss among the rocks. The inclusion in the National Park of the Ossau Reserve, since 1945 classified as a *Réserve Nationale de Chasse*, brings it under strict protection. As hunting is forbidden all year round, the variety of wildlife is

---

In the Magnabaigt valley.

Along the Tour of Pic du Midi d'Ossau.

Col Long de Magnabaigt on the Tour of Pic du Midi d'Ossau.

immense. Instead of reaching for the heights, the Tour leads the walker through the secret ways and quiet valleys of Jean-Pierre, and has a quality that brings you back again and again. It was first marked out in 1966, when it followed a rough plan, crossing the Col de Peyreget. This line is still generally regarded as the official route, but the GR10 makes for the Col de l'Iou and passes south of Pic de Peyreget to provide you with a splendid view of the Anéou amphitheatre and the mountains on the Spanish frontier.

For the advantage of refreshment at both beginning and end, a start at Lac de Bious-Artigues is proposed. There is a small car park, a bar/café and the Refuge Pyrénéa Sports. The car park lies at the end of a narrow and precarious minor road leaving the main Ossau valley just south of Gabas. It soon fills up, and at weekends parking is likely to extend at least as far as the valley camp site north of the lake, adding a kilometre to each end of

---

Plaa de la Quèbe.

the walk. It does not matter which way round you tackle the walk, but an anti-clockwise route begins with an easy stroll, while a clockwise direction calls for a little uphill work early in the day. For this reason, the easier option is described here.

Take the broad path leaving the car park and following the east shoreline of the lake. This is a section of the GR10, and in due course you will ascend along the edge of a pine forest – the Bois de Bious Artigues – above which the dark North Face of Pic du Midi, on which the first rock climbs were developed in 1896, seems to frown down on the little ways of men. Carry on to the Pont de Bious on the edge of the lush green Plaine de Bious. Ahead the eye is drawn to the conspicuous Pic Castérau, while nearer to hand the shallow river sweeps in lazy curves, in no hurry to pursue its downward flight to the great lake below.

The GR10 here disappears, right, into forest again, while the Tour footpath crosses the Gave de Bious and the plain, an ancient glacial lake, for about 800m, before climbing energetically through the Arazures wood (signposted 'Peyreget') in a series of zigzags to emerge in the Peyreget valley, just north of the Cabane de Peyreget, inhabited in summer by shepherds, who are frequently to be found selling their cheeses in the valley below. Here the Tour joins the HRP for a short while, as far as Lac de Peyreget, reached by a gradual ascent southeastwards. You have a choice of routes at this point: either follow the traditional line, over Col de Peyreget, or the GR10, via Col de l'Iou. Between Lac de Peyreget and its Col, where the view of Pic du Midi is rather distorted, there is a devilishly demanding section up past a small tarn and across a boulderfield where the way disappears, marked only by small cairns, amid a chaos of gigantic blocks, and emerges to hit you with a final steep pull to the highest point of the Tour, Col de Peyreget. The plunge downwards, past more tarns, to the blue eye of Lac de Pombie and its refuge seems like child's play afterwards.

Less demanding, though longer, the GR10 tackles the Col de l'Iou leading to a fairly level traverse to the Col du Soum de Pombie. The aspect of the mountain from this easy col is quite breathtaking: it rises dramatically in front of you and gains height as you pursue the gently sloping path downwards to the Refuge de Pombie across grassy glacial moraine.

Beyond the Refuge de Pombie great care is needed crossing La Grande Raillère, as the towering cliffs of the mountain draw your eyes and your attention away from the awkward terrain. Ahead, a sweeping green projection rises abruptly to a pointed peak, Saoubiste. Between the two lies the Col de Suzon, reached by an easy upwards stroll, with towering cliff faces on one hand and rolling, sombre grassy hillsides on the other.

Now you gaze down on green pastures in the outstretched arms of the Magnabaigt valley. This is fairly narrow, with a

---

Pic Saoubiste and Pic de Pombie (right) are prominent landmarks along the Tour of Pic du Midi d'Ossau.

The Crête de Moundelhs, Magnabaigt valley.

Start of the descent into the Magnabaigt valley from Col de Suzon.

major rock step half way down, easily descended by the path, and beyond which I once set to flight a small group of izards – half careering off up the hillside on the left, and the rest bounding down to the lower valley and up the opposite hillside in what seemed like a matter of seconds. Marmots whistle at you from the sanctuary of boulders beneath the Arête de Moundelhs, as the path descends finally into the welcome shade of woodland and the boggy pass of the Col Long de Magnabaigt, rather more of a woodland glade, and an idyllic one at that, than a mountain pass.

On, down, through a canopy of green, the path drops easily to reach the car park at Bious-Artigues, the summits of Jean-Pierre, reappearing high above the trees to signify the end of a remarkable tour.

Time: allow 7+ hours (and enjoy it)

Walk 21 Lac d'Aule (2042m: 6699ft:) and Pic d'Aule (2392m) 7848ft) Grade B/C The ascent of Pic d'Aule, technically easy, nevertheless requires some experience of the demands of steep and rugged hill-walking. The valley of the Aule is fully visible from Lac de Bious-Artigues, rising above forest slopes that are brutally steep. A shorter excursion may be made to Lac d'Aule, saving a good deal in effort, though the first hour would have you doubting this statement.

From the plateau of Bious-Oumettes, near the camp site just north of Lac de Bious-Artigues, descend west to cross the Gave de Bious by a footbridge and set off on a clear footpath that passes above the Cabane de Bious-Oumettes. Very soon it swings to the northwest and climbs steeply up the left bank of the Torrent d'Aule through scattered beech trees. The gradient only eases as the upper limit of the forest is reached. As you leave the trees behind the Crête de Las Becquettes is prominent to the left, a great limestone ridge separating the valleys of the Aule and the Aas de Bielle (Walk 22).

Lac d'Aule: A few minutes after leaving the forest ford the stream and climb to the west for a short distance, until, turning now to the northwest, the path becomes more evident, climbing about 30m above the stream. This leads to the new Cabane d'Aule, on the site of a former cabane, this one well constructed from large rocks.

Above the Cabane continue northwest until the path disappears, and then keep going west up steep grassy slopes, making for a rocky escarpment, which is climbed easily by a shoulder, to find two paths, one above the other, looking down on a steep ravine of collapsed rock; care is needed here. After this awkward passage the path veers progressively towards the west, and reaches some pleasant turf, before leading to a small col beyond which lie the Aule lakes surrounded by steep grassy slopes.

When you have had time to recover your breath the retrospective view of Pic du Midi d'Ossau is especially pleasing, framed in the V-shaped notch of the outflow from the lakes.
Ascent: 1h 30: Descent: 1h

Pic d'Aule: On leaving the forest remain on the left bank, following a path marked in black dashes on the map. The ability of forest to recolonise pasturage from which it was once cleared is particularly noticeable here, as you approach the Cabane d'Aule. Look around and you will notice from the differing heights of the trees where the former forest limits once stood, now extended by a copse of beech and pine. Elsewhere this mountain upland is an expanse of heather, gorse and bilberries, as in Britain, heavily laden with fruit towards the end of summer, and particularly popular with the birds of the forest.

After a short descent, cross the stream and follow the path along the right bank leading to the Cabane. The path now becomes less clear, always remaining on the right bank, and climbing across a landscape studded with low outcrops of rock that often shelter partridge. Higher up, beyond a ravine, there may be grouse or the occasional ptarmigan, though the two are seldom seen together.

On the skyline the Col des Héous is noticeable, and it is necessary to cross a ravine below it to reach a broad hillock to the north of the lakes. From here climb the steep slopes to the Col with care.

From the Col the ridge leading up to Pic d'Aule is steep but not especially difficult.

Ascent: 3h: Descent: 2h 30

Walk 22 Vallon and Col d'Aas de Bielle (2080m: 6824ft) Grade C
The valley of the Aas de Bielle lies to the west of Lac de Bious-Artigues, a lonely secluded place, echoing to cowbells, that will be appreciated by those looking to escape the easier, more populated routes.

From the car park at Bious-Artigues pass round the lake on the north, by a path below the dam wall, to reach a wooded knoll, once a glacial barrier. Go down on to the second barrage and cross it, then follow the northwest edge of the lake for a short distance, crossing two streams, to a broad path climbing steeply into woodland. As elsewhere in this region the forest is principally pine and beech interspersed with small clearings. When a forest trail is encountered, ignore it and continue ahead climbing to the upper limit of the forest and into the upper valley.

On leaving the forest the rising valley suddenly widens, with the Col d'Aas de Bielle directly ahead, to which the path, a long established route, not waymarked but still quite visible, leads. Numerous boulders now litter the way, and a small cabin (suitable for two people in an emergency) has been constructed against one of the boulders.

From the top of the Col there is a superb view across the

Pic Castérau and Lac Roumassot, one of the lakes of Ayous.

---

vallée d'Aspe to Pic d'Anie, Billare, the Massif d'Ansabère, and, more to the south, in Spain, the Pics d'Aspe dominated by Bisaurin (Sp. Visaurin).
Ascent: 2h 30: Descent: 1h 45

It should be possible to make a direct ascent to Pic d'Ayous from the Col, by a steep slope to point 2264m, and then by easy-angled slopes. Though I have not done this myself, such a connection should not be beyond competent walkers, and would facilitate an easy circuit, descending from Pic d'Ayous to the Lacs d'Ayous. (See also Walk 24 for this in reverse).

Beyond the Col d'Aas de Bielle lies the vallée de la Baigt de Saint Cours (Sencours), and an easy descent to meet the GR10, close by a small pond. The waymarked GR10 should then be followed to the Col d'Ayous and a return to Bious-Artigues via the Ayous lakes.
Descent to Baigt de Saint Cours and return via Ayous lakes: 2h-2h 30.

Walk 23 Tour of the Ayous lakes (2103m: 6900ft) Grade C The lakes of Ayous are known for obvious reasons as 'the mirrors of Pic d'Ossau', and the complete circuit visiting each of the lakes is one of the classic walks in the Pyrenees, full of surprises and never failing in interest.

Begin from the Lac de Bious-Artigues car park where a broad trail sets off south, passing the small bar/café (a convenient end of day refreshment spot). There is an immediate sense of anticipation; although the lake is artificial it occupies a splendid site, with Pic d'Aule and Pic Gazier visible at the head of the Aule valley. Immediately south the great northern wall of Pic du Midi d'Ossau rises 700m from the forests below.

The Ayous lakes walk begins easily through pleasant woodland, before climbing southwest around Pic les Aroujos.

Pic du Midi d'Ossau and the Refuge d'Ayous from Lac Gentau.

Continue along the edge of afforested slopes, with spreads of great yellow gentian (*Gentiana lutea*) spilling down on the right of the path, to cross Pont d'Ayous. Climb a little to Pont de Bious, where the great pastureland of the Plaine de Bious suddenly appears ahead with Pic Castérau and Pic Paradis prominent at the head of the valley.

Just before reaching Pont de Bious the path forks, both directions being signposted 'Tour des Lacs'. Either way is acceptable, but anti-clockwise brings you to each lake with little advance warning and a fine element of surprise; by going clockwise, once Lac Bersau is reached, all the other lakes are approached from higher ground, and some of that surprise is lost. For this reason an anti-clockwise circuit is described here.

Take, then, the right fork and start immediately into the welcome shade of pines and beech trees. A steady rise ending in zigzags leads to a clearing before a final skirmish with the forest leaves the path (here both the HRP and GR10 – which says a lot for the quality of the route) to sweep south and west, climbing

Pic du Midi d'Ossau and Pic Peyreget from near Lac Castérau.

easily to the first of the lakes, Lac Roumassot, beyond which Pic Castérau stands in magnificent isolation. North of the lake a fine cascade spills from higher lakes and provides a convenient water supply for the nearby Cabane de Roumassot, invariably occupied in summer, with an entourage of goats, pigs and sheep dogs.

Climb easily beside the cascade to pass north of a smaller lake, Lac du Miey, before continuing to Lac Gentau, overlooking which the National Park have constructed a splendid and immensely popular refuge. Along the northern shore of the lake the path forks, the right branch heading for Col and Pic d'Ayous (Walk 24).

For a while this is the last opportunity to take in the towering

Lac Bersau.

mass of Pic du Midi d'Ossau, often reflected in the lake.

If you can bring yourself to do so, press on south from the Refuge d'Ayous and climb in zigzags and then by a horizontal path through an exquisite string of tiny tarns to the largest of the lakes, Lac Bersau; a small promontory looking across to Pic Hourquette is a delightful spot for a break.

Continuing southwards a col linking Pic de Bielle with Pic Castérau is reached, the latter now presenting a dramatically different profile of vertical cliffs and gullies rising from its own small lake. The suddenness of this view, once more back-stopped by Pic du Midi d'Ossau and its acolyte, Pic Peyreget, and the long undulating frieze of nearby frontier peaks, is justification alone for an anti-clockwise circuit.

The path now zigzags down to pass a deep chasm that consumes the stream flowing from the frontier peaks. Lac Castérau, too, is a popular spot, and the path takes its southern edge, passing another cave before plunging swiftly downwards in wide zigzags, past the Cabanes de la Hosse and the Cabane de Cap de Pount, across slopes decked with Pyrenean iris (*Iris xyphoides*), finally to regain the Plaine de Bious at its southern end. Near the spot where the path used by the Tour du Pic du Midi d'Ossau (which is signposted 'Peyreget') sets off upwards, an area of ground on the left of the path has been taken over by the beautiful blue thistle of the Pyrenees (*Eryngium bourgatii*).

An easy, relaxing stroll across the broad pasture leads to Pont de Bious and a descending retreat to Lac de Bious-Artigues.

Time: 4h 30 (plus a lot of time for stops!)

Walk 24 Pic d'Ayous (2288m: 7506ft) Grade B/C Perched precariously above the vallée d'Aas, the vallée de la Baigt de Saint Cours (Sencours), and the Ayous lakes, Pic d'Ayous is a perfect escape from the throngs to-ing and fro-ing along the HRP, the GR10 and the Ayous lakes walk below. It is an easy ascent from Col d'Ayous, and for that reason is generally ignored.

Follow Walk 23 as far as Lac Gentau, and climb from there to the Col d'Ayous. Follow easy-angled slopes northeast to the summit.

Ascent: 2h 15: Descent: 1h 45

As noted in Walk 22 the northern ridge of Pic d'Ayous to the Col d'Aas de Bielle looks like an eminently suitable way of constructing a circuit, by descending via the vallée d'Aas, but I have not done this myself.

Looking southeast along the frontier from Col d'Anéou. An easy climb on a carpet of flowers leads to Cuyalaret.

Walk 25 Pic Peyreget (2487m: 8159ft) Grade B Pic Peyreget is a prominent outlier to the south of Pic du Midi d'Ossau, an easy summit that justifies a visit for the view it affords of the four summits of Jean-Pierre.

The best approach is from the Anéou car park, north of the Col du Pourtalet to the col west of the Soum de Pombie; this is described in Walk 19, and should be extended as far as the Refuge de Pombie. From the Refuge ascend west on a good, if rugged, path (HRP) to the Col de Peyreget, and from there by easy, trackless slopes to the summit.
Ascent: 2h: Descent: 1h 30

An alternative approach takes the GR10 from point 2129m, west of Soum de Pombie, as far as Col de lIou, and from there with rather more difficulty than from Col de Peyreget, east to the summit.

Walk 26 Col d'Anéou (2243m: 7359ft) Grade C From the car park at the Col du Pourtalet the map shows a number of paths extending westwards across the upper basin of the Anéou amphitheatre, though there is little evidence of them on the ground. Nevertheless, the walk to the Col d'Anéou is an interesting and short excursion, starting off easily but later steepening as the col is approached. The going throughout is on grass that provides pasturage for summer flocks of sheep and goats, and where on two occasions Pyrenean mountain dogs have tried to round up the author along with the sheep.

Behind the hotel at the Col du Pourtalet the start of a path

Descending from distant Col d'Anéou.

The view southwards from Col d'Anéou on the frontier. The prominent peak is the Spanish summit, Pico de Anayet.

The frontier peaks on the approach to Col d'Anéou.

Col d'Anéou.

sets off hopefully, but soon loses its way among a landscape of small hillocks and streamy gullies. The best idea is to locate the valley leading up to Col d'Anéou, rather to the right of the conspicuous tower, the Campana d'Anéous, and just go for it. By following a stream at one point into a narrow and twisting gully some diversion may be made, but gradually the terrain steepens until you are directly below the Col.

Now, with only sheep tracks to aid progress, ascend steadily upwards beneath the Pène de Mauhourat to an upper basin that looks as though it may have held a small tarn in years gone by. Once in this upper section a path may finally be located swinging around the south side and up to the Col, gained rather more steeply than is apparent.

Ascent: 1h 30: Descent: 1h

From the Col, as you step into Spain, the most conspicuous feature is the towering form of Pic d'Anayet and the great wall of Visaurin beyond. Everywhere wild flowers grow in abundance, and here especially you walk on a carpet of *Sempervivum arachnoideum*, well known to rock gardeners and similar in species to the British house leek (*Sempervivum tectorum*).

Pic d'Anéou (2364m: 7756ft), northwest o fthe Col may be ascended on steep grass and friable rock, though an easier ascent may be made by contouring beneath it on the Spanish side to a grassy col and back-tracking from there to the summit. It then becomes feasible to extend the walk over the next summit, Pic de Canaouraoye (2347m: 7700ft) to Col d'Astu and to descend from there in a wide sweep across untracked ground round the Pic de la Gradillère, and by another Col d'Anéou (also known as Col de Bious) back into the Anéou amphitheatre. Shorter is the direct descent from Pic de Canaourouye along the line of the ski piste shown on the map – easy going but long and tiring on a hot day.

The frontier peaks leading to Col d'Anéou.

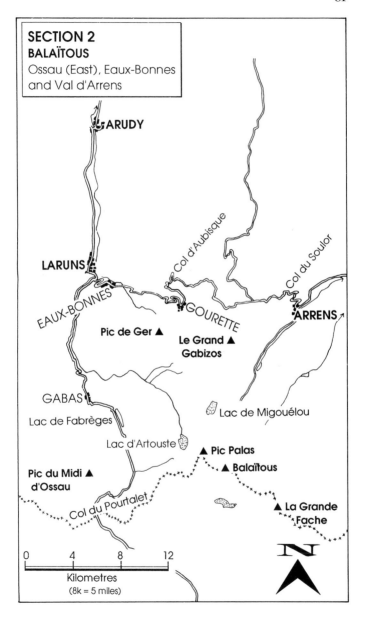

SECTION 2
BALAÏTOUS
Ossau (East), Eaux-Bonnes
and Val d'Arrens

ARUDY

Col d'Aubisque

Col du Soulor

LARUNS

EAUX-BONNES

GOURETTE

ARRENS

Pic de Ger ▲

Le Grand ▲
Gabizos

GABAS

Lac de Migouélou

Lac de Fabrèges

Lac d'Artouste

▲ Pic Palas

▲ Balaïtous

Pic du Midi ▲
d'Ossau

Col du Pourtalet

▲ La Grande
Fache

0   4   8   12

Kilometres
(8k = 5 miles)

N

SECTION 2: BALAITOUS: OSSAU (EAST), EAUX-BONNES AND VAL D'ARRENS

Walk 27 Lac du Lurien (2211m: 7254ft) Grade C This walk is quite demanding, but visits a wild and rugged region generally passed by in favour of more popular and easier attractions.

About 7 kilometres southeast of Gabas in the Ossau valley is the beautiful jade-coloured lake, Lac de Fabrèges. On its east bank something of a minor village has built up serving the Artouste Mountain Railway which clatters for 10 kilometres across the mountains to Lac d'Artouste – a splendid excursion for visitors unable or unwilling to make the ascent on foot (but the track is rather shaded and can get cold, so take something warm to wear).

The ascent to Lac du Lurien begins along this back road, about 100m before the first *paravalanche*, where a slight widening of the road enables a few cars to be parked. The path begins between two low stone walls, climbs above an electricity pylon and aims towards another pylon higher up.

Soon the path enters forest, climbing steeply in badly coordinated zigzags, and seeming to form a divide between stands of pine trees to the north and beech to the south. Gradually the going underfoot becomes more stony and, after having briefly accompanied the Lurien stream, the path clambers to the upper limit of the forest. Now the route enters a narrow valley and climbs as far as a rock outcrop on the other side of the stream, effectively blocking from view the Cabane du Lurien, the only cabane in the region with its own defences against avalanche. If you look nearby you will find the ruins of its predecessor which was not so well protected.

A little higher the terrain becomes more undulating and hillocky and the Lurien glacier of old, here meeting rocks of greater resistance, has had to content itself with a narrow and sinuous composition, rather than the broad, sweeping valleys

Pic Palas (left) and Balaïtous.

Lac d'Artouste, a high and secluded lake, but now easily reached by the Train Touristique d'Artouste from Lac de Fabrèges.

normally associated with glacial action.

Finally, as if determined to erode any remaining stamina, the path rears up sharply to a hollow beyond which, at last, lies Lac du Lurien. There is a certain rugged bleakness about this secluded valley, here in summer you will find many of the limestone-loving plants of the Pyrenees, and in autumn red grouse and ptarmigan, while black redstart and alpine accentor are almost commonplace.

Time: 3h

Walk 28 Col (2259m: 7411ft) and Lac d'Arrious (2285m: 7497ft)
Grade C Begin from the D934 where the road does a kink to pass round the Cabane du Caillou de Soques hillock. There is ample roadside parking here, particularly to the north of the Cabane, and from here a path zigzags up to the edge of forest,

continuing its twisting way in the forest finally to emerge near a bridge spanning the Arrious stream. Now follow the right bank of the stream and climb to and beyond the Cabane d'Arrious with splendid retrospective views to Pic du Midi d'Ossau and the minuscule Refuge de Pombie.

Ahead mountains crowd the horizon as a false col comes into view. The path passes a shelter (of sorts) beneath a large boulder (you would have to be desperate to use it!), and starts climbing in zigzags to reach the first col, an idyllic spot with lush turf and sparkling miniature cascades. The second and true Col d'Arrious, not yet visible, is only a short distance away.
Ascent: 2h: Descent: 1h 30

The view from the Col is rather restricted, not unattractive, but lacking something. Pic Palas, Pic d'Artouste and the Crête d'Artouste are before you, Pic Palas standing on the frontier

Balaïtous (left) and Pic de Lac d'Arrious. The Passage d'Orteig traverses the dark cliff face to reach the boulderfield beyond.

Direction boards are prominent at all main entry points to the Parc National des Pyrénées.

Cabane de Soques, Ossau valley, and the start of the ascent into the Arrious valley.

with Spain which here points sharply northwards before continuing eastwards to Balaïtous.

Yet only a few minutes away awaits a dramatic contrast. By ascending easily south to Lac d'Arrious a vastly more attractive scene opens up. The lake itself first meets you at eye level, its waters reflecting the towering cone of Pic du Lac d'Arrious. But by ascending further left, and climbing to the high point of a small outcrop (a place inhabited by stoat), the view across to Pic Palas suddenly has an immense gulf to contend with, while Balaïtous finally raises its head above the shoulder of Palas to get in on the act. Away to the left the intense blue of Lac d'Artouste draws the eye, its dam and buildings gleaming white.

Refuge d'Arrémoulit

Walkers wanting to continue to the Refuge d'Arrémoulit, have

In upper Val d'Arrious. The prominent peak in the background is the seemingly omnipresent Pic du Midi d'Ossau.

Lac de Fabrèges, Ossau valley.

the choice of descending from Col d'Arrious to just above Lac d'Artouste, and then climbing back up again in broad zigzags to the Refuge, or of tackling the Passage d'Orteig (named after the guide who discovered the route) across the north face of Pic du Lac d'Arrious. This narrow ledge, marked by a dotted red line on the map, is exposed but safe, and is a less tiring approach than the loss of height the alternative route demands. Once beyond the Passage the path (cairned) leads across bouldered terrain and eventually descends to the Refuge.

Walk 29 Pic d'Arriel (Pic Saget) (2824m: 9265ft) Grade B A very elegant and imposing summit when viewed from the vicinity of the Refuge d'Arrémoulit, Pic d'Arriel lies on the frontier and is accessible to walkers with scrambling ability.

The best approach is along the val d'Arrious from the Cabane du Caillou de Soques in the upper Ossau valley. Walk

Lac d'Arrious and Pic d'Arriel.

Pic de Ger from the Col d'Aubisque.

On the summit of Pic de Ger.

28 describes the climb to Col d'Arrious, and this should be followed, but not all the way to the col. Just beyond the rough shelter, the Quèbe d'Arrious, beneath a large boulder the path climbs for a while in zigzags, and then more easily, making for a false col. About 500m after the Quèbe d'Arrious a vague path climbs in zigzags towards the south, then heads southeast to reach the corrie of the vallon de Sobe, north of the Col de Sobe. Ascend to the col, and cross into Spain to follow a track across scree and boulders to the conspicuous Col d'Arriel to the east.

As Col d'Arriel is reached an impressive view opens up of the Cirque d'Arrémoulit and its many lakes. Now climb the frontier ridge southeast to the summit; the ridge is quite steep and involves a little scrambling, but is not unduly difficult and on good rock.

Ascent: 3h 30: Descent: 2h 30

The descent may be varied slightly from the Col de Sobe, by heading north on a path leading to the outflow of Lac d'Arrious. This would prolong the descent by about 45 minutes.

Walk 30 Pic de Ger (2613m: 8573ft) Grade B Pic de Ger is one of the higher summits in the great limestone massif of Eaux-Bonnes that lies south of the western half of the Laruns to Argelès-Gazost road (D918). Most of the summits in this region are modest in height, and the most convenient base for exploration is Gourette, a flourishing ski resort that in summer manages not to look quite as out of place as other similar resorts. From Gourette a broad valley rises to the south, bounded on the west by the Ger ridge and on the east by another ridge rising to Pic de la Latte de Bazen. Between the two, and dividing the upper slopes, is a lesser ridge, the Pène Médaa beyond which the head of the valley is closed by the ridge of the Pène Blanque.

Walkers aiming for Pic de Ger, which holds a fine

commanding position, can elect to walk up the broad pistes from the town, beginning near the *téléski* station, but this is a long and serpentine route, a little confusing in its lower section due to constant rebuilding and rerouting of pistes, and the labour of the ascent adds nothing to the route.

Better to treat yourself for once to a ride on the Téléski de Pène Blanque, which whisks you, with a change of *téléski* halfway, to the upper station at 2376m (7795ft).

On leaving the upper station circle right, around and above it, to locate a waymarked path (yellow and green), heading southwest across the slopes of La Pène Blanque towards the prominent pyramid of Pic d'Amoulat. The path descends slightly for a while, and later forks, with the left branch rising easily to the Col de la Pène Blanque, from where there is a fine

---

Salon de Ger from the summit of Pic de Ger, an uncomfortable but otherwise easy ridge links the two.

view south and southwest, taking in Balaïtous, Pic Palas and Pic du Midi d'Ossau. The more prominent right branch leads to a short section where small boulders and rock outcrops demand care and attention. This then leads to the path crossing the great scree slope of Pic d'Amoulat beneath chough-loud cliffs that rear impressively above you. Contrary to the impression it gives, the path is quite stable, but though in summer little affected by stonefall, this is no place to linger.

At the far end of the slope a rocky knoll, with phallic towers directly above, provides a temporary resting place. These towers mark the approach to the Col d'Amoulat, between that summit and La Pyramide, a small outlier to the north. The path sets off climbing now, aiming for another col, more to the right, the Col du Plaa Ségouné, where the southern ridge of Pic de

Pic de Ger from the Pène Blanque.

Ger begins; the final few metres to the Col can require care in the dry, slippery conditions of summer, but there is ample firm rock to secure your progress. The Col is a delightful place to rest for a while; beyond lies a corrie rising to an intermediate ridge, before the final approach to Pic de Ger.

From the Col descend easily on a prominent path, and later climb by a variety of paths to the intermediate ridge, where the alpine flowers attract an amazing variety of butterfly. A short stroll across this grassy ridge and the path returns to rock for a 'not so steep as it looks' pull to the summit, a neat cairn, with not a lot of room for manoeuvre. Return by the same route.
Ascent: 1h 45: Descent: 1h 15

The view from the summit is quite expansive, taking in Pic du

Pic d'Amoulat. The route to Pic de Ger follows the path, left, crosses the scree slopes and climbs to the right of the pyramid, right.

The continuation from Col du Plaa Ségouné to Pic de Ger.

Midi d'Ossau, Balaïtous, Vignemale and Pic du Midi de Bigorre. A narrow and airy ridge links the summit with Salon de Ger (2611m): 10-15 minutes each way.

Walk 31 Pic de la Pène Blanque (2550m: 8366ft) and Pic Arre-Sourins (2614m: 8576ft) Grade B/C If you take the *téléski* to gain height quickly, then most of the route will be downhill, and while for some walkers that may strike a note of discord, it has to be said that the uphill work is energetic and the long downhill quite splendid. Purists however will find the ascent from Gourette, where the walk begins, to the upper station of the Pène Blanque *téléski* easy enough to follow, in spite of its serpentine and slightly confusing qualities, and adding at least

The view from Col du Paa Ségouné across Col de la Pène Blanque. The line of ascent crosses the scree slopes, bottom right.

two hours to the walk. The start from Gourette leaves by a broad piste near the *téléski* station, and uses the long valley with the Ger ridge on the right (west) and that of the Pène Médaa on the left.

Immediately south of the upper station a steep grassy couloir ascends to a col (2531m), slightly to the east of the summit of La Pène Blanque, from where it is easily attainable.
Ascent: 0h 45-1h.

From the summit, return to the col and continue along the ensuing ridge, easy but narrow in places, to the higher summit of Pic Arre-Sourins. (Time: 0h 45-1h). The view from the ridge is largely of the immediate summits of the Eaux-Bonnes massif; Pic de Ger, of course, is close by to the northwest, while northeast lie the two Gabizos; south the ground drops to the northeast branch of the Soussouéou valley beyond which the prominent summit of Le Lurien may be picked out.

Experienced walkers wanting now to make a speedy return to Gourette will be able to manufacture a steep descent from point 2594 on the ridge, north to Col d'Anglas, and from there by a good path, passing Lac de la Cinda Blanque to the upper station. The continuation of the walk, however, follows the ridge southeast to the Hourquette d'Arre where the waymarked GR10 awaits.

From the Hourquette head northeast, and after 200m pass a hunters shelter near the top of a valley descending east to Lac du Lavedan. The path however continues northeast, crosses a vague col, swings left and then right, before descending in steep hairpin bends to the ruins of old iron mining buildings close to the Anglas lake.

The path passes along the eastern shore of the lake, with a fine view north to the Sarrière ridge, and northeast to the Latte de Bazen. From the lake descend in more steep zigzags to the Valentin stream, and then by pastures, much less cluttered by ski paraphernalia than its westerly neighbour, to Gourette. Descent: 2h-2h 30

Walk 32 Pic du Petit Gabizos (2639m: 8658ft) Grade A/B
Viewed from the plains of the north, the great limestone walls of Pic du Petit Gabizos are among the more conspicuous summits to be readily picked out, in spite of its comparatively modest elevation. It is in fact one of the highest summits in the limestone massif between Eaux-Bonnes and the val d'Azun, and though its 'normal' line of ascent is without any technical difficulty, the poor quality of the rock in its highest reaches demands experience and even a length of rope. Less experienced mortals can still tackle Le Petit Gabizos, but should refrain from pressing on to the summit, however tempting it might seem.

The walk begins from the Col de Soulor on the D918 between Argelès-Gazost and Laruns, an impressive location that has been part commandeered by souvenir stalls, bars and cafés. From here climb the embankment of the road and head generally southwest on a waymarked track (red and yellow) passing a small hill, the Turon de Saucède (1571m), to reach the Col de Saucède. Here cross the GR10 on its great meander and follow a muddy path southeast, later becoming grassy and climbing in zigzags.

When the Las Touergues stream is reached follow it upstream for a minute and then cross to the right bank and ascend roughly south-southeast, gradually moving away from the stream. At about 1580m climb a grassy hillock heading now towards the south-southwest in the direction of the east-west ridge, the Crête de Bassiarey; this is the long descending east ridge of Le Petit Gabizos, and it is reached, steeply towards the end, on a mixture of grass and rock.

The ridge proves to be surprisingly easy, with the summit of Le Petit Gabizos looming ahead, but a small col (2322m), in spite of easy ground beyond it, marks the point from which other than experienced walkers should now retreat.

A short way further the ridge becomes very rocky and demands some rock scrambling in an exposed situation on suspect rock. In one place the ridge narrows dramatically, followed by a pinnacle (turned on the right), but then the difficulties ease and the final steep pull to the summit is blessed with better rock, and as a result is less intimidating.

Ascent: 3h 30: Descent: 2h 30

A return by the same route understandably demands the same degree of caution. Experienced walkers with good scrambling ability can complete a circuit by heading north to the Brèche Edouard and Las Touergues, and then by descending the northeast ridge.

Walk 33 Le Pic du Grand Gabizos (2692m: 8832ft) Grade A/B
The Grand Gabizos (also called Le Pic des Taillades) is the highest summit in the limestone Eaux-Bonnes massif south, east and west of Gourette. From its summit the view is immense, both of the higher mountains towards the frontier regions and of the plains to the north. Its comparatively modest altitude, the rather daunting aspect it presents to walkers, and its position outside the National Park mean that it is often shunned in favour of other heights. Certainly, it is not a walk for the inexperienced, but walkers competent on rock and at finding their way across trackless ground will find Le Grand Gabizos well within their reach, and its final ridge something of an airy and spectacular finish.

The walk sets off from the west bank of the Lac du Tech, reached by the minor road (D105) extending southwest into the val d'Arrens from Arrens-Marsous. Just before the end of the lake, where there is limited off-road parking, a signpost indicates a grassy path heading west-southwest to the Cabane

Pic de Gabizos, seen from the Col de Soulor.

de Bouleste. Very quickly the path enters a small wood, where it wanders about finally to emerge not far from a flight of zigzags that avoid a steep rocky section in the lower vallon de Labas. From the top of the zigzags, the path crosses the hillside, generally towards the west, climbing slightly, and crossing feeder streams until it reaches the Cabane de Bouleste.

From the Cabane, climb north to gain a path zigzagging up a grassy slope to the east of a steep-sided gully. Continue heading north on a cairned path above the left bank of the stream to a level stretch of ground where a number of streams come together. To the west is the Col d'Uzios, but now abandon the path to this col and climb across trackless ground, north-northwest, becoming steeper as a col divided by a pinnacle comes into view. This is the Col de Louesque (2411m), a high rocky pass with an interesting view to the north. Head for this.

Competent walkers with good scrambling ability on reaching the Col will enjoy the rocky ridge to Pic de Louesque and across to a second col (not named on the maps), the Col de Pène Blanque (2540m), then climbing once more all the way to the summit of Gabizos. In fact, strong walkers can make directly for this Col rather than the Col de Louesque, though from below it is not visible: it lies north-northeast and at the western edge of the prominent white limestone cliffs of Le Grand Gabizos. This approach is obviously quicker, but is very steep.

Otherwise, from the Col de Louesque retrace your steps a short distance to cross the southern flank of Pic de Louesque to Col de Pène Blanque. From there the final ridge cannot be

---

The Col de Soulor, a regular crossing on the Tour de France.

avoided, becoming more and more of limestone construction and swinging from a east-southeast direction to east-northeast. Keep as much as possible to the very summit of the ridge along which there are two small cols, but no serious difficulties. The final pull to the summit is rather shaly, and the panorama embraces a catalogue of identifiable peaks – Pic du Midi de Bigorre, Néouvielle, Pic Long, Marboré and the Cirque de Gavarnie, Vignemale, Balaïtous, Palas and Pic du Midi d'Ossau.

Ascent: 4h 30: Descent: 3h 30 (Time may be saved by descending directly from Col de Pène Blanque, though this demands care, and is very tiring).

Walk 34 Lac de Migouélou (2278m: 7474ft) Grade B/C The Lac de Migouélou lies in a vast glacial hollow to the north of the Balaïtous massif. The National Park authority has built a fine refuge here (generally open from mid-June to the end of September), but the fairly demanding approach march tends to deter casual visitors, leaving the place very much to the dedicated Pyrenean wanderer.

From Arrens-Marsous follow the D105 into the val d'Arrens, and continue as far as the Plaa d'Aste, a vast meadow about one kilometre north of the end of the road at the Porte d'Arrens, where incidentally the National Park have a Maison du Parc with a small display of stuffed birds and animals of the region. This is the opportunity to discover how big those griffon vultures really are.

From the road a signposted and waymarked path sets off up an interminable series of zigzags through the Bois de la Mouic, only to find on leaving the forest yet more zigzags await, leading to a small plateau colonised now by wild spinach and sorrel, and a place where a shepherds hut once stood, the Cuyéou de la Mouic.

The path now continues across the lower slopes of the Pic

Arrouy to reach a short stretch that often retains snow well into summer and accommodates a colony of marmots; izards are often seen here, too.

Ahead lies a shallow col beyond which appears the arched construction of the Migouélou dam. There has always been a glacial lake at this spot, but between 1955-8 two dams were built to increase its depth to about 60m to serve the Electricité de France. Working from July to November a team of a hundred workmen was necessary to complete a construction, regarded by some as a work of art!

The lake is very popular with anglers and contains brown and rainbow trout and char. The nearby refuge has 40 places; during its summer opening period, when there is a guardian, it serves refreshments, snacks and full meals. At other times, though part of the hut is left open, there are no facilities.
Time: 3h

Strong walkers who can resolve the transport difficulties may extend their day considerably by continuing northwest from the Migouélou dams to the Col d'Hospitalet, and descending to Lac de Poueylaun and by the vallon de la Lie to the Lac du Tech. Such a circuit would produce a very long day, but with commensurate satisfaction; the Lie valley is renowned for the range and quality of its flowers as well as its wildlife.

Walk 35 Pic de Batbielh (Pic de Batboucou) (2651m: 8697ft) Grade B/C This relatively easy summit, with its grandstand view of the Balaïtous massif, may be reached in a day from the val d'Arrens via the Lac de Migouélou. It would be better, however, to overnight at the Refuge de Migouélou and to make the ascent, refreshed the next day.

Follow Walk 34 to Lac de Migouélou, and from the Refuge take the waymarked path to the southern end of the lake and there leave it to ascend southwards and grapple with a troubled, but easy, corrie dappled with small lakes, Les Lacarrats. Quite often this corrie is still filled with snow into June and July, making progress a little easier.

It is a matter of personal preference whether to aim directly for the summit of Pic de Batbeilh or for the east ridge, ascending from there.

Ascent: (From Lac de Migouélou) 1h 45: Descent: 1h 15

Walk 36 Lac de Suyen (1536m: 5039ft) Grade C/D The beautiful Lac de Suyen lies along the non-motorable extension of the Gave d'Arrens, and is easily reached from the Porte d'Arrens at the southern end of the D105.

Not far from the Maison du Parc National cross the river by a footbridge and follow the wide path along the right bank of the river into forest, where it zigzags upwards before leaving the forest and contouring to the lake.

An old path, still used by those who know of it, keeps to the left bank of the river, and soon reaches the outflow from the lake. Given the two paths, it is a simple matter to effect a short and easy circuit.

Ascent: 0h 30: Descent: 0h 25

Walk 37 Refuge de Larribet, Lacs de Batcrabère (2180m: 7152ft) Grade C The Lacs de Batcrabère lie at the feet of Balaïtous, and this walk is very much a key to the granitic heartlands of the massif. The walk begins from the Porte d'Arrens at the southern end of the val d'Arrens. Just beyond the Maison du Parc National a signposted path sets off for Lac de Suyen, climbing in zigzags through the forest before emerging not far from the lake.

Continue past the lake to a fork at a National Park signboard, and take the path for the Refuge de Larribet. This leads you to a small plateau, a lively place animated by the sound and sight of the Cascade de Doumblas; a small cabin stands nearby.

Marmots have colonies here, izards often come into the valley, while the birdlife is very wide ranging and includes citril finches, crossbills and woodpeckers.

From the cabin cross the stream and pass an old shelter built beneath a large boulder. Now follow a narrow path climbing in zigzags to the tiny Lac de la Claou de Larribet, a beautiful location often nicknamed 'The Japanese Garden'. Here a glacial constriction, a narrow passage highly polished by the Balaïtous glacier, has long been used by shepherds as a barrier preventing sheep and cattle from straying down during the months of summer pasturage.

Once beyond this narrow spot you pass into a large and wild region where the stream meanders attractively, and marmots whistle at you from the rocks. Another rock shelter, the Toue de Larribet, is encountered and then a series of rock steps, nicknamed the 'Ladder of Larribet'. This leads before too long to the very heart of the great glacial cirque of Balaïtous and the Refuge de Larribet.

Having reached the Refuge de Larribet, little more real effort is needed to reach the dramatic Lacs de Batcrabère. From the Refuge follow a path which leads to the Brèche de la Garenère (2189m), a place that can be difficult if under snow, but at other times quite straightforward. The lower lake is soon encountered, while the upper lake involves scrambling around large blocks of granite.

Ascent: (To Refuge de Larribet) 2h 15: Descent: 1h 30
Ascent: (From Refuge de Larribet) 0h 50: Descent: 0h 40

Inevitably, although the lakes are set in an attractive and rugged landscape, it is the great north face of Balaïtous, Pic Palas and Pic d'Artouste that will command greatest attention.

Walk 38 Balaïtous (3144m: 10,315ft) Grade A Balaïtous is rightly counted among the finest and most rewarding of Pyrenean summits; it is no place for idle curiosity or speculative adventure, and demands a high standard of fitness and experience. Almost certainly snow will persist throughout the year, and an ice-axe and crampons are indispensable. Even so, an ascent late in August or September is advised, when most of the snow will have vanished.

The mountain lies in a massively wild, rugged and least accessible region, defended on all sides by adjoining peaks, ridges and great walls of near vertical rock. Many of the early attempts to climb it failed even to reach the lower slopes, while Charles Packe, that knowledgeable pioneer of Pyrenean wandering, spent seven days in 1864 on and around the mountain before finally working out the way to the summit. There, to his surprise, he found a small cairn, proof positive that the mountain had already been conquered. In fact, the first ascent is now accorded to the surveyors, Peytier and Hossard, who after much difficulty reached the summit in 1825, and whose records were misplaced for almost forty years.

These days there are a number of well-defined approaches and ascents, and the bristling ridges of Balaïtous offer varying levels of commitment and challenging routes, all of which benefit from an overnight stay at one of the mountain refuges. Indeed, it would be folly to attempt Balaïtous in a single day expedition unless your fitness and experience is of the highest order; such a day would involve over ten hours of effort, plus rest time. The description that follows makes use of a natural feature on Balaïtous known as the 'Grande Diagonale', and passes the Refuge de Larribet, where an overnight stay is advised.

Begin from Porte d'Arrens and follow Walk 37 to the Refuge de Larribet. Be sure to make an early morning start next day to profit from the cool morning air.

From the Refuge follow the path southwest over the Brèche de la Garénère and descend towards the first of the Batcrabère lakes. The path is part of the HRP, and is followed as far as the lowest of the Micoulaou lakes at 2302m. Col Noir (2625m) on the frontier is now visible to the south, and from the Micoulaou lakes leave the HRP and climb away from the path towards the Col.

The Col Noir is invariably defended by a collar of permanent snow which can become glassy late in the season, making crampons essential. In normal summer conditions this obstacle can be avoided by turning to the right and climbing to the ridge through a chaos of boulders. But even this is not straightforward and may involve some mild scrambling where less experienced walkers may derive comfort from the security of a rope.

Once the Col Noir is gained descend into Spain, losing about 50m of height, down a steep couloir, but generally without difficulty. Once down look for a cairned path leading east to the Abri Michaud (2698m), a natural shelter created beneath an overhanging rock, and 'improved' by a wall of stones, a small window and a door. It would suffice in an emergency.

The shelter is found near the foot of a gully, generally regarded as the start of the ascent proper. Climb this, with a near vertical wall on the right. There is much loose rock here, and though the ascent is not difficult, beware of rockfall should other parties be in the gully. At the top an unexpected grassy platform is reached as the frontier is regained along the broad sloping western ridge of Balaïtous.

From this point a choice of routes is available. Competent scramblers who love messing about on rock should follow a line of cairns on a vague path off to the right (east), gaining height energetically, and reaching a spot where more cairns seem to confuse the issue, offering a number of lines. There is little to choose between any of them; they all clamber along the rocky spine, into gullies and out again, until a final gully, sometimes iced up all year brings you close to the domed summit.

Slightly less demanding, though it doesn't look it, is the Grande Diagonale. From the grassy platform a needle of rock, the Aiguille Lamathe, is seen on the northwest ridge of Balaïtous, and an apparently steep ledge rising diagonally across the northwest face of the mountain. This is the Grande Diagonale.

Turn right from the platform and cross to the foot of this ledge, where you will find it is wider than it looks and less steep. Climb this until about 150m below its head a gendarme is encountered on the left of the ledge. Now look for a cairn which marks the spot where you leave the Diagonale by climbing a wall on the right by an easy gully (providing it is not iced over) to the summit dome. The highest point has a trig point bearing a plaque to the memory of Georges Ledormeur, one of the less-renowned pioneers.

Ascent: (From Porte d'Arrens) 6h: Descent: 4h 30
Ascent: (From Refuge de Larribet) 4h: Descent: 2h 30

Not surprisingly, the summit views are outstanding. A tangled array of ridges, buttresses, and barren hanging valleys lies all around, defending all approaches.

Experienced mountaineers need little cautioning that ascents of this magnitude and complexity often involve descents of even greater difficulty, particularly in the steep gullies and across snowfields. On Balaïtous they can be especially tiring.

Walk 39 Grand Tour of the Lakes and the Refuges Migouélou, Arrémoulit and Larribet (Col d'Artouste 2472m: 8110ft: Col du Palas 2517m: 8256ft: and Port de Lavedan 2615m: 8579ft) Grade B By far the longest walk in this book, the tour of the refuges and the numerous lakes of the Balaïtous massif is for experienced walkers only, a magnificent walk that necessitates overnight stays at two of the refuges. The tour is demanding, and in many of the upper sections snow may be permanent or lasting well into the year, making crampons and an ice-axe indispensable. To be sure of fully experiencing the rugged grandeur of the region a period of settled weather is advisable, and a forecast may be obtained by telephoning 62 32 97 77 or 62 32 90 01.

Day One: Lac de Migouélou: the ascent from the val d'Arrens to the Refuge and Lac de Migouélou is detailed in Walk 34.

As to time of departure, two possibilities suggest themselves; either leave later in the day, after the heat has gone from it, to arrive at the Refuge by about six in the evening, or, better, make an early start, reach the Refuge before midday, and then enjoy a load-free walk to the Col de l'Hospitalet or the Lacs de Lassiedouat.

Day Two: Refuge d'Arrémoulit by Col d'Artouste and Lac d'Artouste: follow the path south from the Refuge de Migouélou above the east shore of the lake. At the southern end of the lake snow often hangs late into summer, but otherwise the route to the Col d'Artouste is trouble-free. From the Col there is a fine view along the vallée de Soussouéou, and it is often possible to pick out the Train Touristique d'Artouste which runs along the opposite flank of the valley.

Zigzags descend from the Col to the Lacs de Carnau, and again normally present no difficulty once the snow has receded. On reaching the outflow of the western lake, cross the stream and follow the easy path leading to Lac d'Artouste. Cross the dam and join the throngs that have journeyed this far by train. Follow the western shoreline of the lake, and at the southern end, at a fork, take the branch climbing left in numerous wide sweeps to find the Refuge d'Arrémoulit nestling among its personal entourage of lakes.

Day Three: Porte d'Arrens by Col du Palas and Refuge de Larribet: the hardest of the three days is also the most rewarding and the most beautiful, crossing briefly into Spain with a fine view of the Lacs d'Arriel, Balaïtous, and the Arêtes des Frondellas.

From the Refuge d'Arrémoulit climb along the edge of the lake on granite slabs for about 200m, until a passage opens up on the left. This is cairned and leads ultimately to the Col du Palas, passing first over a minor col near the Lac de Palas before tackling a boulder slope to reach the Col du Palas itself. Here we stand on the frontier, the Lacs d'Arriel lying below, and the onward route to the Port du Lavedan quite clear across the cirque to the south of Pic Palas (almost always under snow). Aim now for a steep couloir leading directly to the Port du Lavedan.

Cross back into France and descend, always on snow, into the cirque to the north of the Soum de Batcrabère. The path (the HRP, and therefore waymarked) now descends to the Lacs de Micoulaou, Batcrabère and to the Refuge de Larribet, from where a straightforward descent (Walk 37 in reverse) takes you down to Lac de Suyen and the Porte d'Arrens.

Time: Each day will involve between 6 and 8 hours walking, and the walk is easily reversed.

Walk 40 Pic des Cristayets (2723m: 8934ft) Grade B The Pic des Cristayets offers an outstanding and original perspective of the Balaïtous massif, especially of the Glacier de Las Néous and the Crête de Costerillou. That alone makes the ascent worthwhile, but add the obligatory trek into the wild reaches of the upper val d'Arrens, and the combined result is a fine and energetic excursion of the first order.

The walk begins from the Porte d'Arrens at the end of the D105, south of Arrens-Marsous. From here follow the trail leading to Lac de Suyen (Walk 36), but when the path forks south of the lake, ignore the branch (right) to the Refuge de Larribet and continue on a good path (HRP) leading further south into the delightful upper reaches of the valley.

Shortly after the branch (also right) to the Refuge Ledormeur (ignore this, too) climb in zigzags to the Lacs de Remoulis beyond which a vague path heads right, towards the Toue de Casterie (2095m), a rough shelter under a rock. Descend right a little to cross the stream (at spot height 2084) and set off climbing west (pathless) towards the Crête du Diable. The gradient eases in the vicinity of two small tarns, but not for long. From here ascend the steep corrie above, obliquely northwest, toward spot height 2524, and then move west to gain the Brèche de Las Néous (2595m), where the glacier of the same name suddenly springs into view.

From the Brèche ascend an easy slope of grass, flowers and rock to the summit.

Ascent: 3h 30: Descent: 2h 30

Walk 41 Pic Gavizo-Cristail (2890m: 9482ft) Grade B One of the frontier peaks, Gavizo-Cristail offers a striking view of the Crête du Diable, regarded by many as one of the most spectacular granite ridges of the Pyrenees. The view also embraces the southeast face of Balaïtous and the east facing cliffs of the Spanish Picos de la Frondella.

Walk 40 describes the ascent of the upper val d'Arrens, and this should be followed as far as the Toue de Casterie (2095m). Instead of descending right here (as for the Pic des Cristayets), keep faith with the HRP and continue climbing towards the frontier col, Port de la Peyre-Saint-Martin (Col de San Martin on the Spanish side).

From the Col cross to the Spanish side of the ridge and climb northwest on easy slopes (no path as such) up a series of minor rock steps to the summit.

Ascent: (From Porte d'Arrens) 3h 30-4h: Descent: 2h 30-3h.

Walk 42 Pic du Midi d'Arrens (2267m: 7438ft) Grade B Taking its name from the town of Arrens-Marsous some 3 kilometres to the north which it very much dominates, the Pic du Midi d'Arrens is not unduly difficult to ascend, but the slopes are steep and can prove dangerous if snow is still present on the mountain. As elsewhere, the summit offers an excellent vantage point, but its conquest is better not contemplated by other than experienced walkers.

From Arrens follow for about 4 kilometres (2.5 miles) the road which pursues the Gave d'Arrens towards the Barrage du Tech. Near spot height 1060m, about 2 kilometres (1.25 miles) before the dam, a rough track descends to Pont d'Ourey where a few cars may be parked.

Cross the bridge, ignoring a path on the left (which only leads to a barn), and take a grassy path, heading east-southeast and passing beneath electricity cables, and becoming gradually narrower. In a few minutes you pass a small gate giving access to two barns, and shortly the path suddenly changes direction before resuming a course frequently flooded by streams issuing from the hillside. A few yellow waymarkers appear, but these are rather faded and may be missed; keep an eye open for them though, because they mark the line of ascent.

In a while cross the stream, and then recross it a moment later to gain the left bank and then move away from the stream quite sharply, in effect climbing southwest to make a few zigzags before continuing in a southeasterly direction to a small grassy valley. Cross the stream once more and continue along the path, which in summer sometimes loses itself in the grass. Continuing southeast, a solitary beech tree offers a spot for a momentary breather before setting off, ever upwards, to the Cabanes de Mauvèsi, at 1420m. Here leave the path, heading southeast to gain a wide footpath generally ascending east-northeast, finally to cross the Ourey stream at 1643m.

A change of direction takes us north-northeast up a steep grassy slope to height 1682m on a ridge thrown down from the summit, now clearly seen for the first time to the east with, to its right, the minor Pic d'Arrouy. Most of this part of the ascent is grassy, and the path not always evident, but the direction is now obvious.

At about 2030m cross a spur overshadowed by a rock pinnacle known as Monné (2125m), and continue east-northeast, climbing a little more to the edge of a deep ravine rising obliquely to the right (east).

Cross the rock rubble at the top end of this ravine and climb to the base of Pic d'Arrouy, reaching it a few metres below a conspicuous cave.

The next section contains much of the difficulty of this ascent and demands care, crossing a short rocky stretch to gain a steep grassy gully. Numerous stones and rocks make progress

Pic du Midi d'Arrens from the northeast.

difficult, while much of the rock is crumbly and potentially dangerous.

The summit ridge is reached, no doubt breathlessly, at a small col at about 2240m, from which the escape is by a small and easy rock wall, well equipped with holds, and beyond which the crest leads easily to the summit.

Ascent: 3h: Descent: 2h

The only logical way down is to retreat the way you have come, taking great care descending the gully below Pic d'Arrouy, especially if it contains snow. Competent scramblers will have no difficulty adding Pic d'Arrouy and Pic de Mousquès to the day's itinerary, though these should not be attempted by less experienced walkers.

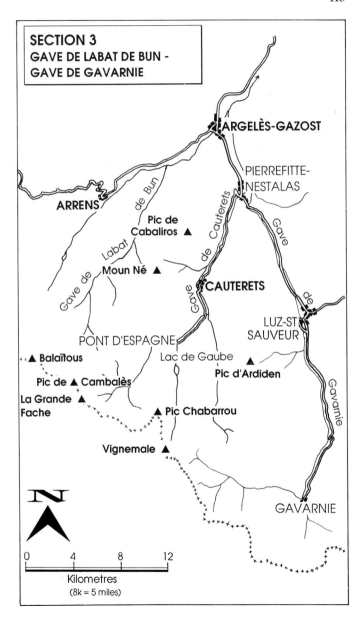

SECTION 3
GAVE DE LABAT DE BUN -
GAVE DE GAVARNIE

ARGELÈS-GAZOST

PIERREFITTE-
NESTALAS

ARRENS

de Bun

Gave de Cauterets

Gave

Pic de
Cabaliros ▲

Labat

Gave de

Moun Né ▲

Gave de Cauterets

CAUTERETS

de

LUZ-ST
SAUVEUR

PONT D'ESPAGNE

Lac de Gaube

▲ Balaïtous

Pic d'Ardiden ▲

Pic de ▲ Cambalès

La Grande ▲
Fache

▲ Pic Chabarrou

Gavarnie

Vignemale ▲

N

GAVARNIE

0   4   8   12

Kilometres
(8k = 5 miles)

SECTION 3: GAVE DE LABAT DE BUN TO GAVE DE GAVARNIE

Walk 43 Lac d'Estaing (1161m: 3809ft) Grade D For many people the lakes themselves are objective enough, and it is rare at the height of the tourist season to find one that doesn't have someone perched on its banks fishing, dangling feet, or paddling in its margins, (swimming is not advised, it's far too cold). Lac d'Estaing is no exception, lying due south of the towering Pic du Midi d'Arrens, along the Gave de Labat de Bun, (D103) which flows through the vallée d'Estaing.

There is a legend that the lake occupies the site of the former village of Estaing which was drowned for turning away a beggar. A poor shepherd who tended his flock from a hut at Estagnet, just east of the lake, took the beggar in for the night and his was the only hut to survive the flooding and devastation in the valley which submerged the village beneath an immense lake.

The tour of the lake requires little in the way of direction, and scarcely takes an hour by any standards. A car park at its southern end is as good a place as any to start and facilitates a leisurely stroll down the road to Pont d'Entounade from where a good path leads via Pont du Pescadou to the northern shore of the lake. With Pic du Midi d'Arrens rising to the north and the long ridge of Pic de Moun Né and Pic du Cabaliros to the east, there is a tremendous sense of being in the very heart of these magnificent mountains, a sensation that will appeal to everyone.

There is also a spread of wild flowers sufficient to satisfy the most accomplished botanist, while the lake is a place to spot dippers, kingfishers, little grebes, and black-headed gulls brought inland by stormy weather at sea. The mountains themselves are home to vultures and eagles, and izard.

Near the outflow of the lake there is a small restaurant known as the Cantine du Lac, a marvellous piece of understatement for a place renowned for its local cuisine.

At the southern end of the lake there is an information centre (*Centre d'Accueil*) with a small bar-café, and from here short walks may be made on signposted routes into the nearby forest which boasts a wide range of hazel, birch, elder, juniper, fir, beech, and spruce, the ideal habitat for pine martin, fox, and roe deer, as well as spotted, black and green woodpeckers, tree-creepers, crossbills, and many finches, including citril.

Above the lake, south from the Pont du Pescadou, a path leads deep into the mountains, along the Gave de Labat de Bun, passing a fine series of cascades en route, which make an excellent and easy stroll, returning the same way. Higher still lie a beautiful group of mountain tarns, less easy of access, surrounded by walls of rock and eminently suitable for a day's excursion (see Walk 44).

Walk 44 Lac du Plaa de Prat (1656m: 5433ft) and the Lacs de Liantran (1824m: 5984ft) Grade C Walk 43 was an introduction to the valley of Labat de Bun, a long and splendid divide into the mountains. Its upper reaches are within the National Park, and here are to be found a host of lakes and tarns, streams and cascades in an exquisite mountain setting, and offering a good and energetic day's walking.

Park at the information centre near Lac d'Estaing and cross the river by the Pont du Pescadou, continuing on a good footpath as far as the signboards which announce your entry into the National Park. The route crosses grass and rocks decorated with holly bushes and numerous species of wild flowers, but is nowhere difficult.

At the Pont de Plasi (1323m) cross the river and follow the ensuing path which zigzags through forest plantations rich in birdlife. On leaving the forest keep an eye open for izards and the marmots which chatter at you from the security of the rocks.

Just after entering the National Park you encounter La Toue de la Cetira, a shepherd's hut constructed beneath a large rock, and in a short while reach the Lac de l'Angle, whose existence depends on the presence or otherwise of snow on the high mountain slopes. A few more minutes bring you to the Lac du Plaa de Prat and its cabin set against the backdrop of the Bois des Masseys.

Here two possibilities face you, either to visit the Lacs de Liantran or the three lakes that nestle beneath the north face of Pic Arrouy. With time to spare both may be accomplished, but the round trip to the Lacs de Liantran, of which there are essentially two, but fed by a number of smaller lakes higher in the cirque, will take about an hour; a visit to the Lac du Pic Arrouy will occupy another four to five hours, to which must be added the hour or so in each direction for the walk between Lac d'Estaing and Lac du Plaa de Prat.

From the latter the shorter walk involves only 155m (500ft) of ascent, while the Arrouy lakes lie as much as 710m (2330ft) higher.

44a Lacs de Liantran From the Cabane du Plaa de Prat head southwest, and in a moment you will find a signpost. The way is well marked and crosses a couple of footbridges, always rising gently until after about half an hour you arrive at a region of enormous granite blocks littering an otherwise grassy landscape. Around the lakes there are the remains of enclosures to protect sheep and cattle against bears (not that you are likely to encounter bears these days, though they are around), as well as small shelters called *cabénères*, in which shepherds kept their milk cool in the chilly mountain waters. Today they are inhabited by a colony of marmots. Return by the same route.

Ascent: 1h 30-2h: Descent: 1h

44b Lacs du Pic Arrouy Pass in front of the Cabane du Plaa de Prat and head towards a small stream beyond which a footpath leads you along the edge of the Bois des Masseys to a fine cascade. The path leads to an open grassy spot with the Cabane des Masseys, like the ruins around the Lacs de Liantran, also colonised by marmots. The path climbs through boulders, heading east, and passes through small plantations of conifers, to reach the first of the three lakes, Lac Nère, set in a deep bowl to the south of an isolated summit, Pic Maleshores. Having gained some height now, there is an impressive view of Balaïtous and its glacier, Las Néous.

Beyond Lac Nère the path climbs once more to Lac Long, and finally, on a less obvious path, to Lac du Pic Arrouy, around which numerous small ponds cluster. To the south rises Pic Arrouy itself, to the northeast, largely screened by an intervening ridge, the even higher summit of Le Grand Barbat. Once more the return is by the outward route.

Ascent: 3h-4h: Descent: 2h 30-3h

Walk 45 Col d'Ilhéou (2242m: 7355ft) and Lac du Barbat (1973m: 6473ft) Grade C The Col d'Ilhéou lies between the massive dome of Pic de Moun Né and Le Grand Barbat, and it is the unrivalled view of the latter that provides the interest in the walk. That you could continue to Lac d'Ilhéou is a bonus, but only for strong walkers who can accommodate the long descent to the lake and the return uphill later in the day; a height variation of 270m (885ft).

Earlier routes have introduced us to Lac d'Estaing and its environs, and it is from here that we follow another route into the high mountains, this time along the GR10, which means that it is waymarked throughout.

It is convenient to park near the information centre not far from the inflow of Lac d'Estaing, and to follow a driveway leading from the centre into the Escale pine forest, until the

GR10 (waymarked) is encountered.

On leaving the forest behind you soon reach the Cabane d'Arriousec, a corruption of *ruisseau sec*, meaning 'dry stream'. For many years this Cabane was occupied by shepherds during the summer months, but now the only attention it receives is from passing walkers. The grassland all around the Cabane, once kept short by flocks of sheep, has now succumbed to stands of holly, hazel and elder trees, a sure sign of the former presence of man.

Beyond the Cabane you cross the forest track which finally ends about 250m further on, and continue along the GR10, for the rest of the route. Rising to the left of the route is the Soum de Grum, directly ahead the Col d'Ilhéou, while to the right Le Grand Barbat easily overtops the intermediate summit, Et-Malh. The pull up the valley is long and tiring, and after crossing the stream by a footbridge, the slope becomes even steeper and the path has to resort to a series of zigzags that take you as far as the Cabanes du Barbat.

From here a short pull, finally leaving the GR10, takes you southwest to a shallow col beyond which the Lac du Barbat is set like a jewel in a wild mountain hollow. Alternatively, another hour of steep walking (southeast) will take you to the Col d'Ilhéou, and the superb spectacle of the Cauterets valley.
Time: (Lac du Barbat) 2h 30: (Col d'Ilhéou) 3h-3h 30

Walk 46 Le Grand Barbat (2813m: 9229ft) Grade B In spite of quite significant ascent (1700m: 5575ft), Le Grand Barbat is neither arduous nor difficult for strong walkers, especially those accustomed to making an early start in the day. The mountain stands apart from the main Pyrenean summits and as a result serves as a spectacular viewpoint. There are two accepted lines of ascent; one from Lac d'Ilhéou, a route not generally along footpaths, and not here described. The other, the *voie normale*, ascends from Lac d'Estaing, an approach using the GR10 for much of the ascent, with the added advantage of affording a return via the lakes below Pic Arrouy and along the Gave de Labat de Bun (Walk 44). For an early start, always advised in the Pyrenees, consider overnight camping near Lac d'Estaing where there is a suitable site.

The route begins by following Walk 45 through the Sapinière de l'Escale, along the GR10 (waymarked by red and white stripes) as far as the metallic green Barbat cabane, shortly before which the GR10 is left behind. In a few minutes the Lac du Barbat is a welcome spot for a rest (1h 45-2h).

Keeping to the east of the lake, climb in a southeasterly direction to gain a higher valley between Et-Malh and the Crête des Mounyolles. This valley has more than its fair share of large testing boulders over which care is needed. Higher still (about 2260m) it forks, one branch heads right, for the Brèche de Badescure, just to the north of a minor peak of the same name; the other, and the one to be followed, climbs left to the Brèche de Barbat, a pull of some 380m (1250ft). This upper section of the route often retains snow well into summer, though the gradient is not unduly steep. Even so, most walkers will appreciate the comfort of an ice-axe, although there are many boulders to haul yourself up by if you don't have one.

The Brèche de Barbat lies southwest of the summit, and about 170m (555ft) below it. From there you can approach the summit by keeping to the left (west) of the main ridge. The way is strewn with boulders, but the angle of ascent has eased considerably and in clear weather presents no difficulty.

To return via the Gave de Labat de Bun, descend to the Brèche de Barbat, and from there move carefully, but without difficulty, down the couloir aiming at the Lac du Pic Arrouy. Unless you want to there is no need to descend all the way to the lake. Keep it on your left, and shortly climb a low ridge west of the lake, and continue descending in the direction of Lac Long. North of Lac Long, and issuing from it, there are a number of small and delightful cascades. Cross the stream below the cascades and reascend a little on its left bank in order to pass a small rock barrier. Lac Nère now lies below you and to the right. Keep it on your right and descend to the path leading to the Bois des Masseys, where you meet the path leading you back to Lac d'Estaing.

Ascent: 4h 30-5h: Descent: 4h 30

Walk 47 Pic du Cabaliros (2334m: 7657ft) Rising as a great dome to the south of Argelès-Gazost, Le Cabaliros is a popular summit, away from the main axis of the range. The mountain is flanked east and west by the valleys of the Gave de Cauterets and the Gave de Labat de Bun, feeding respectively into the Gave de Pau and the vallée d'Azun, which themselves combine at Argelès-Gazost. There are three principal starting points for an ascent, two to the north and the third from the ancient spa and winter sports town of Cauterets. None poses problems for fit walkers, the routes in the main traversing grassy mountain pastureland.

Walkers attacking the mountain from the north will pass through scenery that epitomises the Pyrenean way of life. In the valleys, around the towns and villages the land is devoted to agriculture, the meadows are cultivated, if only to produce sillage. Above the villages the forest takes over, and above the forest rise the summer pastures where shepherds still spend the summer months with their flocks, living in the many cabanes that dot the landscape.

The Pic du Cabaliros is very much a focal point for the communes in its surrounding valleys, notably those of St Savin, Arras, Sireix and Arcizans-Avant. Along the ridge towards Moun Né shepherds used to be permitted to gather together their errant flocks without the risk of seizure or fines, on condition that they returned them safely to their proper pastures *de sol à sol*, that is to say, between sunrise and sunset.

Often they were up on the mountain all night, trying to locate their cattle and sheep . . . as if shepherding didn't have enough problems!

All is pasture now, but Le Cabaliros has suffered a bout of mineral mining, mostly for lead and zinc, initiated by the Spanish Société Penarroya in 1898, and later British interests who extended the extraction north, towards Arras and Sireix. The minerals were transported across the mountains by an aerial cableway that extended for some 15 kilometres to crushing mills in Pierrefitte-Soulom. All the posts and iron bars needed to construct the cableway and for use in the mines had to be brought up on the backs of mules, and in one respect at least little has changed, for mules are still used during the summer months to transport the belongings of shepherds up and down the mountains to their summer homes. The mining however

Approaching Pic du Cabaliros.

only lasted about twenty years, and had ended by the start of the First World War.

47a From Sireix Grade C Two hundred metres north of the village a minor road sets off into the Bois de la Coste before swinging back above the village to begin a serpentine passage through the Bois de la Curadère. This forest trail (La Route Forestière de la Curadère), metalled for half of its length, runs for 10 kilometres (6.25 miles) through the forest to reach a grassy plateau at about 1680m, near a minor bump, Pouy Droumidé. The metalled half of the trail becomes progressively potholed and broken, while the latter section is rocky, rutted and in a ruinous state, but still motorable with care.

From the end of the trail, with Pic du Cabaliros rising impressively across the intervening gulf, a path sets off across pastureland towards the northern end of a long grassy ridge thrown down by the mountain. Just to the north of a minor top, La Tucoy, the path is joined by the route from Arcizans-Avant (Walk 47b), and from here both walks share the same line of ascent.

Follow the path which passes La Tucoy on its western flank, and in due course you will reach a dilapidated line of pylons, part of the aerial cableway used by the lead mines. Behind the pylons rises the grassy dome of Pic Arraillé, and this is the start of the long ridge which will ultimately lead you to the summit of Le Cabaliros. The path up Pic Arraillé is not clear (not that one is really needed), and it is easy to be tempted into following a much more conspicuous path keeping to the west of the ridge. There is nothing wrong in this, in fact the path explores some very pleasant hollows, in spring full of wild flowers. As you near Cabaliros, not far from a small lake that in summer retains little water, you are forced upwards to join the ridge for the final half kilometre, meeting it just north of the Soum de Lat Dessus.

But, on a clear day, it is much more satisfying to keep to the crest of the ridge and to follow this over Le Malinat to the Soum de Lat Dessus, where for a final few minutes the ridge narrows dramatically, rocks pierce the grass, and a long side ridge plunges down to the Gave de Cauterets. A path guides you precariously through this hiatus to begin a final pull to the summit, on which there is a topograph to aid identification of the surrounding mountains.

Ascent: 2h 30: Descent: 1h 30

The final ridge to the summit of Pic du Cabaliros, before cloud totally obscured the view.

47b From Arcizans-Avant Grade C The Route du Cabaliros, in part used during August for a race up the mountain, begins 200m west of the village, and winds its way for 13 kilometres (8 miles) across the broad northern slopes until it reaches a narrow col southwest of a hillock, Turon de Bène. This 'road' is motorable, but only just, and in places there is a real risk of grounding family cars. At best it will prove a nasty shock to their system, and my advice is only to use this approach in vehicles suitable for off-the-road use, preferably four-wheel drive.

From here a grassy path swings west and south around the head of the eastern flank of the hillside above the Gave de Cauterets. In a few minutes it meets the route ascending from Pouy Droumidé (47a), and shares with it the remainder of the journey. The ascent and descent times are the same.

47c From Cauterets (Mamelon Vert) Grade B/C Cauterets is a holiday spa resort at the head of four high valleys, a thriving community of great interest, with unrivalled waterfalls that provide a magnificent spectacle. Much attention is given now to the demands of winter sports enthusiasts, but in the literary world of France it is almost legendary, thanks largely to the works of Marguerite de Navarre, George Sand, Alfred de Vigny, Chateaubriand and Victor Hugo.

From Mamelon Vert, a suburb just north of the town, follow the winding road to Igau farm (shown, but not named on the IGN map), at 1098m, where it is possible to park a few cars. Here you will also find a small café (d'Haoumède). Beyond the farm a new track has extended the route for a short distance, and near the end of this the former track from the Igau farm should be joined as it sets off roughly northwards towards a fence. Here take a path that goes around a group of barns (de l'Espone) and cross the side stream (de Bourg Débat) at about 1450m. Now the path climbs north and northwest to the edge of the Bois de la Peyre, an isolated part of the greater forest which once cloaked these hillsides.

With a sense of relief a short horizontal section is reached before the path crosses the stream (de Catarrabes) and starts a series of zigzags, gradually approaching the main ridge above, but passing below one tempting col (de Caucestre) before making tracks, northeast, for another col (de Contente). The ridge is gained a short distance to the east of the true col, and the path passes round a small knoll.

Once on the ridge the feeling of openness is tremendous; the Pic de Moun Né and Le Grand Barbat rise impressively to the south, the summit of Le Cabaliros is now only a short distance away, and on either flank steep mountainsides drop to the valleys below.

The final section of the ridge is gained near a ruined building at the Plaa de la Termi, once a *hôtellerie*, known to local inhabitants as the Cantine du Cabaliros, and to which the guides of Cauterets used to transport *curistes* (ie those who came to Cauterets to take the spa waters, though it is tempting to think of a curiste as a 'curious tourist'). The journey was made on the backs of mules and lasted about three hours. If that didn't cure you, nothing could!

Beyond the now ruined hotel the crest dips to the Col d'Anapéou, with the lake of the same name nestling perfectly in the hollow below. Now all that remains is to follow the crest to the summit. Generally, this splendid vantage point will provide you with a moment's peaceful contemplation, but, alas, so potent is the drawing power of Le Cabaliros, that its ascent, especially from Cauterets, has become a classic for both summer and winter visitors, and company never seems far away.

Ascent: 3h 30: Descent: 2h 30

Walk 48 Pic de Moun Né (Le Monné de Cauterets) (2724m: 8937ft) Grade B Rising due west of the town of Cauterets, it is not surprising that Moun Né has long been a popular ascent. During the last century society ladies and gentlemen were regularly transported to the summit in chairs. Should you choose to follow in their footsteps you cannot fail to be impressed by the stamina of the porters, for Moun Né has an ascent of 1470m (4820ft), and its initial slopes are steep.

Much of the porters' path still remains, if occasionally overgrown, but it is sufficient to guide you safely to the summit in clear weather. The final stretch however is a little confusing in mist, and if visibility is in this way restricted, it is wiser to leave the mountain for a finer day.

The starting point is a small footbridge across the Gave de Cambasque not far from the intermediate station on the Téléphérique du Lis; motorists should leave Cauterets heading for Pont d'Espagne, but at the southern end of the town take a winding minor road, La Route du Cambasque, which climbs ultimately to an enormous ski car park at Le Courbet. As you approach the cable car station, with an electricity transformer on the left of the road, turn sharply right on to a wide and rough (but motorable) track descending to the bridge across the Gave de Cambasque. There is limited parking near the bridge, rather more near the turning.

Beyond the bridge a track continues past a number of barns and later forks, the right branch going to La Ferme Basque. Ignore this, keep left and start to climb steeply first north and then west by a long series of zigzags up a vast grassy slope also covered in ferns, basically heading for the Cinquet stream, and passing the Bois de Guédot en route.

This same position may be reached rather more directly by strong walkers from about 50m beyond the bridge across the Gave de Cambasque. The stream (Le Cinquet) here descends a steep grassy gully, and a narrow path climbs the gully, very steeply for about 15 minutes with a barbed wire enclosure on your left, until you can conveniently cross the steam and join the path ascending from La Ferme Basque.

Throughout most of the ascent the summit of Moun Né rises above you, mocking, but undeniably beckoning. From the Bois de Guédot a long gradually ascending traverse leads southwest then west-northwest to rejoin Le Cinquet at about 1700m. More zigzags follow, reaching (at 2070m) a grassy ridge (La Crête de Mans Arrouy) separating the route from the vast hollow of the Cirque du Lis. The path does not cross the ridge, but starts to move away from it, towards the north. Yet more zigzags bring you to face the final pull to the summit, stony underfoot now, and demanding care. The path crosses debris fallen from the flank of the main ridge, and then a rocky ravine, finally joining the crest at 2680m. At first the path avoids part of the crest, but later rejoins it, following it in fine airy fashion. Walkers affected by the steep drops on both sides of the ridge will find a more comforting path a few metres down on the right (as you face the summit). Both approaches are without difficulty, and bring you to the immense panorama afforded by the summit.

Ascent: 4h: Descent: 3h.

Walk 49 Pic de Péguère(2316m: 7598ft) Grade B In spite of its comparatively modest elevation, the Pic de Péguère, rising dramatically to the southwest of Cauterets, has something of a reputation for claiming lives. It lies sandwiched between the Gave d'Ilhéou and the Gave de Cambasque to the north and the wooded val de Jéret, and with little more than two kilometres separating the two valleys, plus a height gain of more than 1000m, it requires only a modicum of ability to figure out that its sides are steep . . . and therein lies the problem. In fact, from the val de Jéret to the summit is a horizontal distance of about one kilometre and an ascent also through 1000m, in other words a gradient of almost 100% (1 in 1). Fortunately for walkers a less abrupt ascent has been contrived to ease the agony, and by delaying an ascent until the end of June at the earliest you will (usually) avoid the compacted snow that lingers on the northern flank, the cause of all the problems.

The starting point is the Pont du Ceriset, about one kilometre into the val de Jéret, after the turning to La Fruitière. Just after two hairpin bends a track descends on the right to the Pont du Ceriset, where there is room to park a few cars. There is also room to park alongside the road, and this has the advantage of shading the car from the afternoon sun.

For a while the Cascade du Ceriset will command your attention, often pluming water high into the air to form miniature rainbows. Finally, cross the bridge to meet the Sentier des Cascades (Walk 50), across which a wide path sets of northwards to the first of the 76 bends that await you.

It is my experience that going at these steep ascents like a bull at a gate will have you flagging long before halfway, while a mechanical plod, pausing often for a drink, taking in the scenery, watching the birds that fill these wooded hillsides will foster steady progress.

Although Pic du Péguère lies northwest of the starting point, the general direction of the ascent is north, and passes en route a forester's hut (about 1h), a cableway used by foresters (1h 45) and, a few minutes later a small shelter where the retaining walls are in an advanced state of collapse but represent little danger to walkers. Half an hour later another shelter, also in a bad state of repair, is encountered, but from it there is a splendid view of Cauterets to which the northern slopes of the mountain plunge dramatically.

Shortly, the path passes around the northeast face of Le Petit Péguère (Péguère N.E.). The onward route is more or less horizontal, but for a while in poor condition.

Another ten minutes brings you to a small terrace (2045m) on the north spur of Le Petit Péguère. Here a change of direction takes you southwest, more or less contouring along below the summit ridge. The route is now waymarked by red paint, and it is imperative that it is followed meticulously to the summit. It is along this stretch that a number of fatalities have occurred, but in summer conditions the ascent should present no difficulties.

Like virtually all of the higher Pyrenean peaks the view is quite tremendous, but Le Péguère offers an especially impressive view southwards over the Lac de Gaube to the great north wall of Vignemale.

Ascent: 3h 30: Descent: 2h

River detail along the Sentier des Cascades.

Walk 50 Sentier des Cascades (1496m: 4908ft) Grade D This
delightful walk through the Péguère Forêt Domaniale
(National Forest) is enlivened by the cascading waters of the
Gave de Jéret. The forest is a fine example of 19th century
forestry practices designed to protect vulnerable valleys and
villages from the havoc of floods and avalanches; it also
maintains a richness in the soil which otherwise would be
flushed away by the streams spilling from the hillsides.
Composed mostly of beech and pine, the forest is alive with
wildlife, including the shy izards and many species of birds. This
walk is best done in springtime and early summer, when the
river flows with raging meltwater, the flowers are at their best,
the forest at its most serene, and high season tourism not yet in
full swing, essential if you are to catch sight of anything of note.

The route requires little description, following a good path
(GR10) between the mountain village of La Raillère, just south
of Cauterets, and the Pont d'Espagne, always on the true left
bank of the river. At the southern end of the village, just before
the bridge, a path ascends into the forest opposite a thermal
hotel (des Griffons), renowned for its sulphurous waters which
spring from the hillside just above the hotel at a constant 46
degrees.

The first waterfall you encounter is the Mauhourat, a spot
favoured by dippers that plunge nonchalantly into the raging
water. Through much of the forest the floor is littered with
boulders of all shapes and sizes, fallen from the steep slopes of
the Pic du Péguère above; most are ancient, but each year more
tumble down, especially in winter as fragments of rock are
prised from the cliff face by the constant process of thawing and
freezing. For the rest of the year the danger is a nominal one,
though you need to be alert to the possibility of stonefalls . . . a
raillère is, after all, a scree slope.

Next comes the Cascade d'Escane-Gat, and a short distance
on, the Cascade du Ceriset. Just above this waterfall, near a

bridge, a path sets off, right. This is the start of a demanding and energetic ascent of the Pic du Péguère, largely screened by the forest, that dominates the val de Jéret, an ascent best left to the fit types of the hillwalking fraternity (see Walk 49 if the prospect intrigues you). On the opposite side of the bridge a small monument commemorates the activities of one of the great forestry engineers of this region, Prosper Demontzey, a man who at the end of the 19th century was largely responsible for much of the protective forestry work mentioned earlier.

As you climb higher along the path you enter a region favoured by the older of the male izards, who come in the heat of summer to seek the coolness of the forest shade. A few zigzags are needed to ascend above the Cascade de Pouey-Bacou, quickly followed by the Cascade (and bridge) du Pas de l'Ours (bear's footprint). Folklore relates how a lumberjack from Cauterets was chased here by a female bear so large that in jumping the river it left its paw prints in the rocks. You might, of course, wonder how such a large bear could possibly jump the river at this point, but why spoil a nice story with such trivia? Nearby, particularly around the bridge and along the river banks, you will find quite a few large hollows (*marmites de géants* – literally, giants' pots) scoured by the action of swirling rocks carried in the water.

Further upstream you reach another bridge (Pont de Boussès), near a small island named after the celebrated actress Sarah Bernhardt, who so loved this spot that she often camped here.

The path now relaxes as it enters an open, grassy clearing between the river and the forest. Shortly, the ascent is resumed, climbing easily in zigzags to reach the top of the Cascade de Boussès from where the way runs alongside the river on a kind of raised embankment paved with slabs of granite to protect it from the worst of the river's erosive force, while a short way on, as the path moves away from the river, there is a fine example of rocks worn smooth by the action of ancient glaciers more than ten thousand years ago.

Finally, the route returns to the river for the remaining stretch to the Pont d'Espagne, placing you conveniently close by an excellent bar-restaurant-hotel.

Ascent: 2h

Walkers needing to return to La Raillère will find that the quickest way is down the road; with more time, and after suitable refreshment, you could go back the way you came, and pleasurably, too.

Descent: 1h 15

Walk 51 Lacs de l'Embarrat, Lac du Pourtalet and Lac Nère (The Circuit of the Lakes)(2429m: 7969ft) Grade C One of the finest circular walks in the Pyrenees, this tour is an excellent introduction to the sort of remote wandering and day-long walks that are the mainstay of these mountains for those with no pressing desire to climb to the highest peaks. Reaching 2429m (7969ft) at its highest point, the whole of the walk is confined to valleys and follows clear pathways throughout.

Begin from the main car park at Pont d'Espagne, and immediately cross a footbridge over the Gave du Marcadau to follow a metalled roadway to the open Plateau du Cayan. At a National Park information board ignore the prominent track going left (this is the way by which you will in due course return), and head instead half right to cross the river once more by the Pont du Cayan. It is perfectly feasible to reach this bridge from Pont d'Espagne by the opposite (true left) bank of the river, though the length of the day to come favours a brisk start along the road.

Once across the Pont du Cayan ascend left on a track climbing into a forest of pines and conifers. This next section of the route is steep, but the gradient is eased by a series of zigzags and good views of the Cascades d'Embarrat and east to the Massif de Gaube and beyond.

On leaving the forest you cross a bouldery section to a small grassy plateau and the ruins of a shepherd's cabin. Here a rich carpet of wild flowers adds colour to the landscape in spring and early summer, while overhead you may catch sight of golden eagles or griffon vultures as they patrol the mountains in search of the dead or dying . . . so keep moving!

The path swings to the south to pass round a small hillock before reaching (at 2076m: 6810ft) the lower of the two Lacs d'Embarrat (literally, the 'enclosed lakes' – and well named for the valley in which they rest is a hanging valley, suspended high above the main valley of the Marcadau, and all around towering peaks gather their grey walls protectively, La Cardinquère and Mont Aigu to the south, Les Aiguilles de Castet Abarca and the Pic Arrouy to the north).

Not far from Pont d'Espagne the Gave du Marcadau meanders across stony beds before the mad cascade to the valley below.

It is a simple stroll from Pont d'Espagne to Pont du Cayan, but the bridge also allows access to the Lacs de l'Embarrat.

The lower lake seems quite deep, while the upper, reached by a stony path crossed in spring by a number of streams, is quite the opposite and bordered by upland pastures that provide sustenance for the summer herds of cattle and sheep whose bells add plaintive accompaniment to the sound of running water and the incessant chirping of crickets.

From the upper lake the path continues, climbing westwards to a fork. Ignore the path going right, and take instead the path leading to Lac du Pourtet, which is reached shortly after a small cascade spilling from its outflow. This is the highest point of the walk, and from here virtually all is downhill. The lake is particularly interesting geologically, unique in fact, because its waters serve two valleys: the one by which you have ascended, and also the Marcadau by means of underground passages that have a resurgence just above Lac Nère.

From the lake the route, passing down its east flank on a mini cliff path, descends through a small rocky valley beneath two fine peaks, La Habassole and Mont Aigu, to reach Lac Nère.

The lower and larger of the two Lacs de l'Embarrat.

This lake, too, is passed on the east. About one kilometre further south the path is joined by the HRP, passing from the Col de Cambalès (west) to the Col d'Arratille (southeast), and this demanding high level route across the Pyrenees is shared as far as the Refuge Wallon. The Refuge Wallon is a remarkable construction in a remarkable setting, truly a place to refresh the soul, and eminently accessible along the Marcadau valley (see Walk 52), the route that now completes the circle to the Pont d'Espagne. The Refuge is inaccessible by road, and stands at an altitude of 1865m (6120ft). It is generally open from mid-June to the end of September, and provides a restaurant service as well as overnight accommodation. There is a pleasant chapel nearby, and walkers who discover the urge to explore further in this region could do worse than use the Refuge Wallon as a base.

Below the Refuge an array of signboards indicate the way to

The lower of the Lacs de l'Embarrat and the crenellated ridges of the Cauterets massif beyond.

Pont d'Espagne, but allow yourself a few moments to take in the long Arratille valley and the ring of summits, prominent amongst which is La Grande Fache (southwest).

The path along the Gave du Marcadau needs no description, it is clear and well worn and climbs first through a spread of Scots pines before following the river to the Pont d'Estalounqué. Here the path leaves the river for a while and passes through woodland before dropping to the plateau around the Pont du Cayan. Now is the time, if you still have the strength, to use the path on the true left bank of the Gave du Marcadau to Pont d'Espagne.

Time: 6h-7h

Walk 52 Refuge Wallon (1865m: 6119ft) and the Marcadau valley Grade D Barely three kilometres (2 miles) from the frontier, the Refuge Wallon is a popular base from which to climb the great ring of peaks that encircle it. But the pleasures of this remote sanctum can also be sampled by those who simply want a pleasant and easy walk from Pont d'Espagne.

From the western end of the car park at Pont d'Espagne a prominent path leads out across the Plateau du Clot and beneath a conspicuous couloir, Le Lit Sarrouère, with a reputation for winter avalanches. On the slopes rising above the river izards can often be found early in the morning or during spells of cold weather.

The path is never in doubt and brings you to the Pont du Cayan where you cross the Gave du Marcadau. To the south the broad Marcadau valley can be seen to continue, but the path leaves the river for a while to ascend easily through woodland before dropping to the Pont d'Estalounqué. The name, possibly derived from *étang allongé*, meaning a 'long lake', suggests that a lake once filled the picturesque valley plateau beyond the bridge many years ago. At the end of this plateau a short steep rise raises the path a notch to pass through a group of

Scots pines growing, it seems, from fissures and crevices in the underlying granite.

Soon the path reaches the confluence of the Gave d'Arratille and the Gave du Marcadau. Beyond rise the mountains of the frontier, but in one respect this meeting of the waters is a frontier in its own right, for it marks the limit of the cantons of Panticosa (in Spain) and Saint Savin. Grazing rights here belong to the French only until the end of July, when they pass to their Spanish neighbours until the end of the year. The allocation of these rights of pasturage, a relic from the days when much of the Pyrenees was formed into self-governing mountain kingdoms, takes place every three years at a meeting of representatives from both nations.

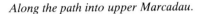

Along the path into upper Marcadau.

From this confluence a short ascent west leads in a matter of minutes to the Refuge Wallon. The Refuge is also known by the name Refuge du Marcadau (literally, 'a market place'), signifying that this place was, until the beginning of the twentieth century a market place used by the Spanish and French.

Not far from the Refuge there is a small chapel built in the 1960s by the abbot of Pragnères, a Bigourdan, a celebrated ecclesiastic, mountaineer, hunter and sometime poacher, a person whose memory remains very much alive among those who knew him.

Each year, on the 5th August, a pilgrimage is made in memory of those who have perished in these mountains, setting off from the Refuge Wallon to climb to the summit of La

The walk into Marcadau from Pont d'Espagne is a pleasant and uncomplicated affair.

The Refuge Wallon (Marcadau).

Pic Arraillous is a prominent peak west of Refuge Wallon.

Glimpses of tree-flanked torrents are just one of the many delights of the Pyrenees.

Grande Fache. That this remote region has long been inhabited by man is evident from the plateau opposite the Refuge, where there are numerous prehistoric remains – burial chambers, stone circles, sepulchral chambers and tumuli.

Clearly, it seems the Port du Marcadau, at 2541m the lowest crossing of the frontier hereabouts, is a long established thoroughfare, of great importance in prehistoric times, and the whole of this remarkable hinterland a scene of man's early development on earth.

From this ancient sanctum the return to Pont d'Espagne is made by the same route.

Time: 5h

Walk 53 Gave de Cambalès and the Cambalès lakes Grade D
The Refuge Wallon is an admirable launch pad for a number of relatively easy walks into the valleys that radiate from it. Each valley possesses its own characteristics, though they have all been fashioned by glacial action during the last Ice Age, about 10,000 years ago. The journey from Pont d'Espagne to Refuge Wallon and back generally takes between four and five hours, and this time has to be added to the time given below for the ascent along the Gave de Cambalès. Walkers wanting to visit all the valleys should consider the advantages of staying at the Refuge for a few days: if it is a sense of remoteness you want, nothing could be better.

From the Refuge the HRP climbs steadily northwestwards, passing through a beautiful and very old pine forest, several hundred years old if the gnarled appearance of the trees is anything to go by. At a small grassy plateau, Pé det Malh (2053m) it changes direction, heading west, and leaving the path north to Lac Nère which is the route of Walk 51 in reverse.

A series of zigzags eases the ascent as you surmount a broad slope which for the moment conceals the hanging valley of

Cambalès beyond. Once across a small col (2252m) the valley and its lakes start to open up before you. To the left another smaller hanging valley contains the amazingly green Lacs d'Opale, though I have yet to discover any opals for myself.

The HRP continues ever westwards to the Col de Cambalès (2706m: 8877ft) from where there is a splendid prospect of Balaïtous. Unfortunately, the chaotic state of the cirque wall, often with snow still clinging to it even well into summer, and numerous large boulders strewn everywhere, makes the final part of the ascent to the Col a precarious undertaking. With care it should present no serious difficulty, but there is a greater likelihood that the lakes in the valley below will prove a sufficient objective. The map shows only about thirty of them, but almost very nook and cranny holds water, and in the heat of the day you may well discover that paddling your feet is preferable to pounding them.

Ascent: 3h: Descent: 2h

Walk 54 Lacs and Col de la Fache Grade C As with all the walks in this great upper region of the Marcadau the Refuge Wallon (Walk 52) is an admirable forward base, and to gain full advantage from this idyllic location walkers are recommended seriously to consider staying at the Refuge overnight prior to tackling any of the walks. The alternative is a day prolonged by the five hours or so spent to-ing and fro-ing between the Refuge and Pont d'Espagne.

The ascent to the Col de La Fache is without difficulty, and is perhaps the most straightforward of all the walks setting out from the Refuge Wallon, though it serves as part of the HRP.

From the Refuge descend southwest towards the stream where you will find a footbridge hidden behind a rocky outcrop. The Col de la Fache is quite prominent to the west, though from time to time it will become obscured by rocky buttresses and hillocks. Cross the stream and continue on a path climbing easily across mountain pastureland to two more footbridges across minor branches of the Marcadau. After the second of these leave the attractive Plateau de Loubosso on your left and climb in zigzags, heading west.

At about 2190m there is an easing in the gradient for a while before it becomes necessary to pass round a pinnacle of rock (2360m) on its south side. Shortly after the path cross a stream issuing from a delightful lake nestling in a hollow on your right; this is the first of the Lacs de la Fache. Ahead a sort of col appears, at about 2460m, just north of the two main lakes.

On reaching the col, continue westwards into a stony depression. Now the true Col de la Fache is plainly in view ahead of you. The final section is not difficult, but is often still under snow well into June. The Col reaches an altitude of 2664m (8740ft).

Not surprisingly the view across the frontier is breathtaking, and is what makes the ascent worthwhile. Immediately below you are more Lacs de la Fache with the HRP picking a way through them, pressing on into the heart of the Spanish mountains between the great Circo de Piedrafita and the Picos de la Frondella, themselves rising dramatically to the great tower of Balaïtous. While in the middle of this massive valley the Lac Darré-Spumous (Ibon del Respumoso) cannot fail to catch the eye.

Ascent: 2h 30: Descent: 1h 45

Walk 55 La Grande Fache (3005m: 9859ft) and Pic de Cambalès (2965m: 9728ft) Grade B The scene each 5th August of a pilgrimage from the Refuge Wallon, the ascent of La Grande Fache is not an unduly difficult undertaking. Strong walkers could make the return ascent from Pont d'Espagne in a long day, though an overnight stay at the Refuge is a better idea. The key to the ascent is the Col de la Fache, and this may also be used to climb the Pic de Cambalès to the north.

Walk 54 to the Col de la Fache is followed for the two and a half hours or so it takes to reach the Col from where a path climbs due south, slightly to the right of the frontier crest. Nowhere is this difficult, nor does the ridge itself present any problems, though care is needed to avoid stonefall and loose rocks. Two small brèches are encountered just before the summit, which should be reached in about one hour from the Col.

For the Pic de Cambalès walkers must head north from the Col de la Fache, first to negotiate an enormous pile of rocks that assumes the name, Pène d'Aragon. Beyond, the line of the frontier is followed (northwest), clambering easily over blocks, not all of which however are stable, and demand caution.

From the Col d'Aragon, continue due north, still on slightly

La Grande Fache from the Refuge Wallon.

unstable granite blocks, but now on the Spanish side of the main ridge. After about ten minutes there is a tremendous and abrupt view through a break in the ridge of the Glacier d'Aragon and the Lacs d'Opale. About one and a half hours from the Col de la Fache (30 minutes from the Col d'Aragon) is needed to reach the summit. As with La Grande Fache, the view is quite remarkable, and strong walkers should be able to combine both summits in a single trip of about 9 hours.

Walk 56 Port du Marcadau (2541m: 8336ft) Grade C The lowest of the high mountain passes giving access to the upper reaches of the Marcadau from Spain, the Port du Marcadau, has a long history as a well established thoroughfare. A 'port' in this sense is a wide col. Yet in spite of its fairly modest elevation, the climb to the Port du Marcadau is an energetic pull, becoming more demanding the closer you approach the frontier ridge.

For a while the route shares that for the ascent to the Col de la Fache, setting off southwest from the Refuge Wallon to locate a footbridge concealed by a rocky outcrop. Continue across upland pastures and cross two more branches of the Marcadau, also by footbridges. After the second of these the path to the Col de la Fache climbs westwards in a series of zigzags, but the route to the Port du Marcadau now pursues its own stream across the Plateau de Loubosso. At 2040m the gradient sharpens dramatically and begins a long series of zigzags, crossing and recrossing streams which flow from the vicinity of a small lake, Hount Frido (2230m), after which you thirst, or munch on the snows that lay claim to this north-facing slope well into summer.

At the Col a great bowl of water awaits, alas out of reach. For here a large hanging valley retains a number of richly green reservoir lakes, the Lacs de Pecico, feeding the great expanse of the Embalse Alto de Bachimaña and its dam to the south.
Ascent: 3h: Descent: 2h

Walk 57 The Arratille valley (2528m: 8294ft) Grade C The ascent of the Gave d'Arratille to its lake, and ultimately, its col, is rather more demanding than the other similar walks that fan out from the Refuge Wallon. It is still well within the capabilities of most regular walkers, but the valley is just that little more wild, just that little more rugged, the evidence of the cataclysmic struggle that produced the range of mountains millions of years ago that bit more pronounced. From the col, however, it will be the dramatic mass of Vignemale that draws the eye, rather more than the folded, sun-scorched landscape of the Spanish side.

Entrance into the valley leaves the approach to the Refuge Wallon at a National Park signboard, a little above the confluence of the Gave du Marcadau and the Gave d'Arratille. A path descends to a footbridge across the Arratille, shortly followed by another by which the true right bank of the stream may be gained. Gradually, the path gains height, passing through a series of thinly wooded undulations to reach a wide glacial basin where a range of large granite slabs bear witness to the passage of glaciers that once filled these high mountain valleys.

A short way further the path suddenly rears steeply to traverse a massive rock step, only accomplished by several steep zigzags. Beyond, the valley narrows dramatically, and a few last pines clinging to the mountainside mark a discernible transition from sub-alpine to alpine conditions.

Soon the Lac d'Arratille appears, and as you cross the footbridge over the stream issuing from it you leave the difficulties behind for the moment. The bridge actually spans a geological fault, marking a great shifting of the earth's crust about 290 million years ago. A little further the lake itself appears, and invites a measure of relaxation in an impressively rugged setting.

More geological evidence awaits as the path continues from a region of granite to one founded on sedimentary rocks which was formed during the Palaeozoic period, about 400 million years ago.

The path runs alongside the lake and passes round a deep cove, beyond which a spread of enormous limestone boulders marks the limit of the small glacier, formed during the last Ice Age, which fashioned the Lac d'Arratille. Geologists have shown that this glacial tongue sprang from the Pic de la Badète d'Arratille and the Petit Pic d'Arratille, summits which form the skyline to the southwest.

Once across this region of geological frontiers the path (the HRP) becomes better waymarked and cairned, but not for long. To the right of the path a few shallow lakes of crystal clear water gather, fed by the outflow from the higher Lac de la Badette. Continuing south the terrain once more changes abruptly; this time the grassy patches leading to the head of the valley have been replaced by a massive boulder field. Many of the boulders are unstable, but a steep series of zigzags makes progress easier.

Finally, beneath the col, lies the Lac du Col d'Arratille, a lake of the deepest blue sparkling water, contrasting intensely with the grey rocks all around. This upper section of the valley is very narrow, and snow clings to the rocky slopes well into summer, but at 2528m, the Col d'Arratille is only a few metres higher than the lake, and easily reached.

Once on the Col d'Arratille, Vignemale, some 770m (2525ft) higher still, dominates everything, while below the wide valley of the Rio Ara spills downwards to the distant Spanish plains.

Ascent: 3h 30: Descent: 2h 30

Across the Col the HRP curves around the head of the Rio Ara to the Col des Mulets, beyond which it drops back into France to the Refuge des Oulettes de Gaube. Very strong walkers could make a magnificent day for themselves by setting off early in the morning from Pont d'Espagne and heading via Marcadau and Arratille to the Gave des Oulettes, and from there to the Lac de Gaube and back to Pont d'Espagne. About 10 hours of walking (plus stops); quite an undertaking (Grade B/C).

Walk 58 Lac de Gaube (1730m: 5677ft) Grade C/D Walkers visiting the Pyrenees for the first time will enjoy a real flavour of these mountains on this brief and uncomplicated walk. The route begins at the Pont d'Espagne, half a kilometre beyond which there are two massive car parks; there needs to be, because Pont d'Espagne is the starting point for a good twenty or so routes into the mountains, and even this brute fills up early in the day, especially during July and August.

Return from the car park towards Pont d'Espagne, taking time to admire and photograph the Gave de Marcadau as it plummets through a very narrow gorge, and locate a National Park information board a short distance beyond, on the right. A track (signposted 'Lac de Gaube' and 'Refuge des Oulettes') heads, initially steeply, up through beautiful fir trees. The path, part of the GR10, is waymarked throughout and leads uneventfully to Lac de Gaube, with the scenery improving as you ascend.

The lake springs upon you rather suddenly, though at the height of summer it will be anything but quiet, for there is not only a splendid lake here, but a bar and restaurant, and little reason to go any further.

Ascent: 1h: Descent: 0h 40

By retracing your steps a little you can cross the outflow of the lake by a broad wooden bridge and follow a path along its western shore. This path takes you deep into the inner sanctum of Vignemale, past the Splumouse waterfall, to the Refuge des Oulettes. To continue in this way will require at least another two hours, during which the whole character of the terrain changes, becoming more rugged, more wild, and less tolerant of the plastic sandal and picnic brigade you will have left behind at the lake.

Walkers returning to Pont d'Espagne need not retrace their steps through the fir plantation below the lake, but can follow a broad path from the outflow which leads to a *télésiège*. Leave this as the terminal comes into view (you are likely to meet the queue first) and descend by a track initially doubling back, but then sweeping downwards to the Marcadau. The path is clearly marked on the map.

Descent: 0h 40

Walk 59 Pic Chabarrou Nord (2925m: 9596ft) Grade A The valleys of the Marcadau and the Gaube are separated by the vallon du Pouey Trénous, the enclosing walls of which later join and continue south as a narrow ridge rising to meet the frontier at Pic Alphonse Meillon. A little way along this linking ridge, and not much lower in height than the frontier ridge, lie the two Chabarrou peaks.

The more the valleys become thronged with summer visitors, the more strong walkers look to the heights for escape. And in the Pic Chabarrou Nord will be found a fine, if demanding, retreat with a grandstand view of the highest summit along the frontier, Vignemale. The start of the walk is shared with one of the most popular short walks in this part of the Pyrenees, but as you progress further into the stronghold of the high mountains, it is with the companionship of rocky walls, snowfields, boulder slopes and the sound of cascading water.

From Pont d'Espagne Walk 58 will lead you first to the popular Lac de Gaube. From here you cross the outflow by a wooden bridge to gain the western bank of the lake along which runs a waymarked path, part of the GR10. At the southern end of the lake do not take the first bridge on the left, but a little further on, cross the Gave des Oulettes de Gaube by a second bridge situated just below a small gorge from where there is a fine retrospective view of the lake. The path immediately climbs to the Cabane de Pinet.

A little over a kilometre further a sharp rise at the Splumouse waterfall leads in a few minutes to a footbridge across the stream, the gradient now a little easier. Beyond the bridge the path moves steadily away from the stream, and after circumventing a stretch of boggy ground near the Cascade Darré Splumouse, climbs a small escarpment to reach the northern end of the Petites Oulettes plateau. Facing you in all its glory is the towering north face of Vignemale, a scene to move every walkers heart.

At the northern end of the plateau the hard work begins as you leave the path, climbing steeply to the west, heading for the unseen Lac du Chabarrou. A less prominent path appears, marked by cairns, and climbs in zigzags to the outflow of the lake (2302m). Due west now rise the pyramidal slopes of Pic Chabarrou Nord.

Continue along the northern edge of the lake until you can start to pass round it on an indistinct footpath picking a way through boulders. A narrow path cut into the rock walls leads round to the western edge of the lake, from where you ascend west-southwest, no longer aided by a footpath, and as much by guesswork as anything else, but without difficulty. Your direction should be towards the conspicuous brèche high above you, Entre-les-Chabarrous, though it is not necessary actually to climb to the brèche, in fact to do so then necessitates an ascent of the south ridge of the mountain, something best left to walkers who are also competent on rock climbs. At about 2760m you reach a rocky barrier, to the left of which there is a couloir giving access to the brèche. The couloir retains snow well into summer, though it is not especially steep.

From the couloir climb right (northwest) across awkward

boulder slopes to reach the jagged crest of the ridge at about 2900m (9515ft), some 25m below the summit. A return by the same route is advised.

Ascent: 5h: Descent: 4h

Walk 60 Vignemale Grade A At 3298m (10,820ft), Vignemale is the highest summit actually on the frontier between France and Spain; it is also the only mountain with any real semblance of a glacier, though modest by Alpine standards. In essence it is not one summit, but a ring of summits, all higher than 3200m, and between them they offer experienced mountaineers a wide choice of routes.

The mountain was first ascended in 1837 by two guides out planning a new route for a client. Both guides contrived to fall into the Grande Crevasse, at that time the major obstacle on the Ossoue Glacier, but by a series of labyrinthine corridors between ice walls they managed to find a way out of the glacier and on to the mountain, finally scrambling to the summit. A year later a quite indomitable woman from Halifax, Anne Lister, teamed up with one of the guides and made the first 'tourist' ascent of the mountain, from the Ara valley in Spain. For many years this was the recognised route up the mountain, a choice founded very much on an understandable fear of walking on glaciers.

Twenty-four years after the first ascent of Vignemale there began one of the weirdest associations between man and a mountain when Count Henry Russell, an eccentric gentleman of Irish/Gascon descent, made his first of at least 33 ascents. With many ascents of Pyrenean summits to his credit, including winter ascents, Russell sought ways of remaining on the mountain without the need to descend to the valleys. His first endeavour was to spend a night in a shallow grave on the very summit. Then he built a series of grottos along its flanks. His seventh and final grotto, which he named Le Paradis, was constructed only a few metres below the summit, and in his seventieth year he made his final ascent of the mountain, spending some seventeen days here. Often in his 'homes from home' he would entertain visitors, stage dinner parties attired in full evening dress, and once arranged to celebrate mass there. So great was his devotion to the mountain, and so widely known, that in 1889 the four summits of Vignemale were leased to him for a term of 99 years for a mere one franc per year.

The highest point of the mountain is known as Pique Longue, and its north face, peering down the Gave des Oulettes de Gaube, offers rock climbs of great length and severity. The Ossoue Glacier is now accepted as the easiest line of ascent, and generally presents no problems, though this is not an ascent to undertake alone or without proper equipment. It is feasible to reach the summit from a valley start and return in the day, but

The upper Ossoue valley, by which the distant Vignemale massif may be reached.

such a demanding undertaking is not recommended when two quite fine and strategically placed mountain huts are on hand.

The key hut is the Refuge de Bayssellance, perched high at the head of the Ossoue valley, just below the pass of Hourquette d'Ossoue. It is accessible either from Gavarnie by the Ossoue valley or from Pont d'Espagne by the vallée de Gaube in which is found the second hut, the Refuge des Oulettes de Gaube.

The Refuge de Bayssellance (Club Alpin Français), the highest refuge in the Pyrenees, is a rather basic hut with self-cooking facilities, it has about 60 places and is open from 1 July to 15 September. The Refuge des Oulettes de Gaube (also CAF) remains open from 1 June to the end of September, and has 80 places and self-catering facilities. The walk to the Bayssellance hut takes about 4 hours from the dam of the Ossoue lake. About the same time is needed to reach the

Along the Ossoue valley: Piméné is the distant peak.

Oulettes de Gaube hut from Pont d'Espagne, but to that must be added two hours to cross the Hourquette d'Ossoue and descend the short distance to the Refuge de Bayssellance.

Approach to the Refuge de Bayssellance from Gavarnie: On the left as you enter Gavarnie there is an excellent bar-restaurant, La Ruade. Just opposite, a road heads into the mountains, making for the border at the Port de Boucharo, but at the first bend leave it, right, for a narrow road leading into the Ossoue valley. The road is in reasonable condition for about 4 kilometres (2½ miles), following which another 4 kilometres of less amenable surface takes you to the Ossoue lake. From here a grassy path (GR10) continues up the valley on the north side of the lake for one kilometre before crossing the stream. The upper valley narrows, and the path bears right above a gorge before descending a little to rejoin the stream. Usually at this altitude there are permanent patches of snow, and the path goes right, across them to join a path climbing northwards. In spite of the presence of snow the path is obvious, and climbs in numerous zigzags to pass beneath three of Henry Russell's caves, the Grottes de Bellevue. The hut is about one kilometre above the grottos, but is not obvious until you are level with it. There are a number of tracks leading up to it.

Approach to the Refuge de Bayssellance from Pont d'Espagne: Though longer, this in my view, is the better of the two approaches. The ascent to Lac de Gaube is detailed in Walk 58, while the continuation towards the Refuge des Oulettes de Gaube is substantially covered in Walk 59. In any case, the path throughout the length of the valley is so prominent that there is no danger of losing it, nor much need of description.

From the Refuge the path (still the GR10) starts to head southeast, climbing above a plateau that looks like it might once have held a lake. The path is a good one, and popular during August and September, though possibly still retaining snow any earlier than that. A long series of zigzags leads to a junction with a path climbing to the Col d'Arraillé. Here, take the right fork, crossing large areas of scree and frozen snow before climbing to the Hourquette d'Ossoue. The Refuge de Bayssellance lies about 600m away down the eastern slope.

The ascent to the high point of Pique Longue from the Refuge de Bayssellance involves a (usually) straightforward walk up the glacier followed by an easy scramble to the summit. Some of the old accounts of ascents of Vignemale depict a rather more substantial and complex glacier over 100 years ago, and there are quite a few tales of people falling into the many crevasses. Now, in normal summers all the crevasses are safely covered by snow, and a well trodden path leads to the foot of Pique Longue.

Descend from the Refuge towards Gavarnie for a short distance to Point 2550, where a narrow path leads off (west) towards the glacier, crossing more or less horizontally a steep scree slope issuing from the Crête du Petit Vignemale. Beyond this you descend half left to the rubbishy ground below the snout of the glacier, where a track, usually compacted snow, passes under the end of the glacier. This is not a place to linger, for there is a real risk of rock and ice falls.

As the snout of the glacier varies according to season it is not easy to be precise about the point of entry, but there will have been others before you, and their trails will show the way. The lower part of the glacier is quite steep, and may justify wearing crampons.

Once on the glacier the general direction is up it, rather right of centre, until the gradient eases and you reach the level of the upper basin, where the full ring of Vignemale peaks comes into view: north, Pointe Chausenque (3204m); northwest, Pique Longue; left of Pique Longue is the Pic du Clot de la Hount (3289m), while to the west rise the Pic de Cerbillona (3247m) and the Pic Central (3235m).

From the upper basin bear half right to the foot of the rocks of Pique Longue and scramble as the spirit moves you easily to the summit.

Ascent: 3h (from the Refuge). The descent is about the same.

NOTE: In some seasons the crevasses may open in late summer, or earlier if winter snows have been light, and it is always advisable to consult the guardian at the Refuge as to the state of the glacier. If it looks like being a problem, you can still reach Pique Longue by crossing beneath the glacier to gain the Crête du Montferrat, following this on the glacier side of the crest until you are level with the upper basin, when it should be possible to cross.

Walk 61 Petit Vignemale (3032m: 9947ft) Grade B The ascent of Petit Vignemale by its northern ridge is an excellent

The Ossoue lake, looking towards Petit Vignemale and the Hourquette d'Ossoue.

A quiet corner in the Ossoue valley.

Soum Blanc de Secugnat rises sharply along the northern flank of the Ossoue valley.

introduction to the high mountains along the frontier little more than a kilometre away. Its northern ridge is a fine airy ascent, well trodden and tending to keep to the left of the main line of the ridge.

The key to this ascent is the high mountain pass, the Hourquette d'Ossoue, from where little more than a hour will be needed to reach the summit. The Hourquette may be reached either from Pont d'Espagne or the Barrage d'Ossoue (Gavarnie) by either of the approaches described in Walk 60.

Unlike its higher and mightier sibling, the Petit Vignemale can be accomplished in a long day without the need to stay at a refuge. From Pont d'Espagne about 7 hours are needed for the ascent, and 4-5 to get back down again. From the Ossoue dam the time can be reduced to 5 hours for the ascent and 3-4 for the descent. Such prolonged activity, however, involving considerable ascent, is very demanding and calls for a high level of fitness. It should not be contemplated by anyone less than fully fit.

Walk 62 Vallée de Lutour (1804m: 5919ft) Grade D The vallée de Lutour is the third and most easterly of the trio of valleys that spread south from the town of Cauterets. Less picturesque than Marcadau (but then what isn't?), and less imposing, perhaps, than the Gaube, the Lutour is no less a sparkling valley penetrating the granite mountains to a fine lake set against the backcloth of an impressive cirque, while the summits that dominate its length lack none of the allure of higher mountains. Also very much in its favour, it is invariably less frequented, especially above La Fruitière.

From La Raillère, an attractive village, rather given over to souvenir shops, and poised precariously below massive boulder slopes, a path leaves the road at the first bend after the Pont de Benquès and climbs easily southeast towards a prominent waterfall, the Cascade de Lutour. Soon the path reaches a footbridge spanning the Gave de Lutour just below the waterfall and gives access to a path that climbs in zigzags to meet at 1186m a second path which follows the true right bank of the river to the small café, La Fruitière, on the left bank and reached by a bridge.

Beyond La Fruitière, having returned to the right bank, the path continues to a cabane, and later you cross to the opposite bank by means of the Pont de Pouey-Caüt. Gradually, with the fine cirque of mountains at the head of the valley increasing in stature, you come to the Lac d'Estom where there is a small inn, usually open from mid-June to mid-October.

Ascent: 3h-3h 30: Descent: 2h 30

Walk 63 Pic d'Ardiden (2988m: 9803ft) Grade B It is the last quarter of this ascent, negotiating a difficult crest of unstable boulders, that places L'Ardiden in the province of experienced walkers only. Moreover, there is a formidable ascent of some 1700m (5575ft) to take into account. Walkers who do tackle it, however, will be well rewarded; wanting only another 12m of altitude to join the elite '3000' club, Pic d'Ardiden, with its vast and impressive panorama, is unquestionably one of the great mountains of the Pyrenees, and far less frequented than the others. Lying between the Lutour valley and the valley of the Gave de Pau the summit is a prominent landmark, and a long, rough walk.

Begin from La Fruitière café in the vallée de Lutour, where there is room to park cars, and cross the bridge to gain the true right bank of the Gave de Lutour. Follow this southwards, soon climbing a small rockstep called the Portail de Limouras and later reaching a shelter, the Cabane de Pouey-Caüt. After about one hour the path crosses a side stream, the Lanusse, and immediately forks left to climb the Sentier Falisse (signposted) to the Refuge Russell, something of a basic hut under the control of the Club Touring de France, but with few amenities.

The ascent is quite arduous and zigzags ease the gradient through the forest.

From the Refuge (1980m) follow a path heading southeast for the Col de Culaus, but leave this after about 500m for a faint and intermittently-cairned track heading northeast through a vast boulder field. After several twists and turns the path heads north towards an obvious col, the Pourtau des Agudes, part way down the southwest ridge of L'Ardiden.

Continue ascending until you reach the Col, a broad saddle (2566m), cross it and continue ahead for about 10m, then bear right to follow the tormented ridge, mostly loose and broken boulders, many unstable, to the summit. A line just to the left of the crest seems easiest, but here the emphasis must be on security rather more than the aesthetics of route-finding.
Ascent: 5h: Descent: 3h 30

Walk 64 Pic de Cestrède (2947m: 9668ft) Grade B Like its rival, Pic d'Ardiden to the north, Pic de Cestrède is a rough and rugged mountain involving the traverse of vast regions of loose and unstable boulders, and best left to walkers experienced in this kind of difficult terrain. We all have to learn somewhere, of course, how to tackle such difficult going, but the mountains that lie between the vallée de Lutour and the Gave de Pau are not the best place to start.

As far as the fork in the path, about 500m beyond Refuge Russell, this and Walk 63 share the same way. When the route for L'Ardiden goes left, you continue ahead along a cairned path that meanders in and out of an enormous boulder field in which, in spite of the cairns, it is easy to lose ones way. If you do, your objective is the prominent Col de Culaus, though you may have to climb on to one of the boulders to see it. Remember, too, that this upper section of the ascent is void of streams, so on a hot day be sure you are carrying plenty of liquid before committing yourself to it.

From the Col head southwest, starting up a crest initially quite broad and not too steep, though all that soon changes. Soon, the ridge narrows quite dramatically, with steep drops on either side, though such obstacles as there are can be passed without difficulty, usually on the right. Before long the ascending ridge meets another (2861m) about 300m northeast of the summit. The intervening ridge is rather scrappy, not very wide and rather exposed in places necessitating scrambling skills, but nothing more. When you do reach the summit the view embraces the distant massif of Néouvielle to the east, the huge limestone bulk of far off Mont Perdu, the third highest summit in the range to the southeast, and, much nearer, the towering cliffs of Vignemale to the southwest, with Balaïtous beyond. Quite spectacular.

Ascent: 5h: Descent: 3h 30

Walk 65 Soum d'Aspé (2968m: 9737ft) Grade B At the height of summer in the Pyrenees it is difficult to avoid people. Everywhere you go, even quite high in the mountains, you will encounter someone, whether a band of the serious-faced *alpinistes*, or a few less determined souls happy with a jaunt to a mountain lake or a distant col. But an ascent of the Soum d'Aspé, approaching along its valley from the east, raises the odds on the novelty of solitude just a bit. The route is generally without difficulty, but best attempted only by experienced walkers. Even so, a simple stroll up the valley will give most people a flavour of this idyllic retreat.

Lying north of the popular vallée d'Ossoue track, and gained only by a twisting mountain road rising from the village of Gèdre, the Aspé tends to be overlooked. The approach from Gèdre follows a minor road, leaving the N21/D921 at the first hairpin bend south of the village, for Saussa, then continuing further to park about 300m after the Pont de Saugué.

From the bridge continue west on a rough road, past some

barns and then climb slightly left to gain a path heading west and keeping its distance from the valley river. The ascending slope is quite gentle, the route more or less following the line of a former irrigation channel. Eventually the path descends to meet the river, and then moves away again to avoid some marshy ground and to climb a small rocky hillock at the foot of limestone cliffs. This is one of the increasing number of haunts in which you could find marmots, their ability to multiply evidently having a lot in common with rabbits!

Once beyond the cliffs the path descends slightly to a small plateau and in a few minutes reaches the Cabane d'Aspé (1848m). Now cross the stream and climb northwest, no longer on a footpath, and with the pyramid of Malh Arrouy ahead of you. The going underfoot is grassy and rather steep, but presents no difficulty. Ahead there are outcrops of rocks through which you should pass, now heading north-northwest towards the Col de l'Oule. Just below the level of the Pique Cadières you should change direction and head west into a region of small plateaux and rocky hollows. As you arrive due south of Malh Arrouy and north of an isolated peak, Pic de Béou Corn (2666m) you reach a wide and rocky basin rising sharply to the Crête d'Aspé above. Head now for the obvious col just west of the Pic de Béou Corn and from there climb the ridge to the west and then northwest, generally left of the crest, but essentially by guesswork to avoid the worst of the chaos of rocks and boulders.

The summit is now due west, and it is not necessary to continue up the ridge to a minor summit (2916m) at the junction of the ridge with the Crête d'Aspé (unless you want to). Instead leave the ridge and pass around the head of a small cirque, aiming for a col north of the Soum d'Aspé. Everywhere the going is rugged and wild, and many of the boulders unstable. The final pull to the summit is steep but not difficult, and the crest marks the boundary of the National Park.

From the summit there is a spectacular view of the Cirque de Gavarnie, the Ossoue Glacier and Vignemale, and the lakes of Estom Soubiran.

Ascent: 4h 30: Descent: 3h

Walk 66 Le Pourteillou (2381m: 7812ft) Grade B/C One of the most remarkable vantage points of the region, yet significantly lower than many of the surrounding summits, Le Pourteillou is an excellent test, if you need one, of whether you have what it takes to tackle the various Grade B walks that are included in this book. The summit, if you can find it, lies along a fairly narrow and steep-sided ridge to the east of the shapely Soum Blanc de Sécugnat, and isnt even identified on most maps. For this reason, and the need to negotiate a vertical wall of rock immediately below the true summit, the walk ends at the Pourteillou col, a beautiful, comfortable and sheltered spot that, to be honest, you wouldnt want to leave anyway!

Leave Gavarnie by the road opposite La Ruade bar-restaurant and at the first hairpin bend take the minor road into the Ossoue valley. After about one kilometre a variant of the GR10 crosses the road, near the Pont de Saint-Savin, and heads east at an angle, passing under a high tension cable before curving round to pass a hillock, Turoun de Tési, by a grassy saddle (1574m).

Once across the saddle descend easily northwards, more or less along the line of the high tension cable. Before too long however start ascending left across mountain pastures linking the spot heights 1641, 1871 and 2040. Initially this is rather steep, but becomes easier. By the time you reach the vicinity of the last height the Pourteillou col appears up on your left, not immediately obvious, but identified by the prominent reddish tinge to the rocks to the west of it.

Heading towards this brèche, along the line of a skiers piste (traced in blue on the map), you climb a short, steep rock step surrounded by large boulders to a narrow break in the ridge above, and then, finally descend slightly to the west by means of a small valley to a hollow beneath a vertical wall of rock. Experienced walkers may feel like tackling the wall of rock, but otherwise this pleasant spot, sheltered from most winds, with its incredible panorama, and a savage plunge to the Gave d'Ossoue at your feet is as far as you need to go.

Ascent: 2h 30 : Descent: 1h 45

Walk 67 Pic de Viscos (2141m: 7024ft) and Soum des Aulhères (2168m: 7113ft) Grade C To anyone driving down the Gave de Pau from the direction of Lourdes the shapely cone of the Pic de Viscos is a prominent landmark. Behind it, running south, lies a long grassy ridge extending to (and beyond) the rounded Soum des Aulhères. Linking the two summits is a fine and for the most part an easy walk, but with a few moments of precarious passage as you near the summit of Viscos.

The key to the ascent is the minor road leaving St Sauveur and ascending to the ski station at Luz-Ardiden, from where you continue to the parking area at Bédéret. Being a winter location the minimal facilities, toilets, bar-restaurant, etc. that exist here are usually closed for much if not all of the summer months.

From the parking area, it is possible to pick out to the west-northwest the Col de Riou, and this is the first objective. Energetic walkers could simply walk straight up to it, but others will find no difficulty following the twists and turns of the arrangement of broad trails that eventually find their way to the Col. The precise line of these does not accord with the maps, though this is of no consequence, and even the vaguest sense of direction will get you to the Col.

From the Col, with its immense view westwards to Cauterets and the distant peaks of Cabaliros and Moun Né, the Soum des Aulhères is a simple grassy stroll southwest, and should take only 30 minutes in each direction.

On the Col there are the ruins of a former hotel, now a forlorn sight, and behind them will be found a path leading north along a grassy ridge. The path skirts most of the minor bumps along the way – Pène de Bassots (2012m), Escalabor (2048m), Pène Nère (2058m) and Tuc des Arribans (2088m) – to arrive, just after the Soum de Counques, at a short descent across very friable ground at the head of a steep ravine and this has a fair sense of exposure about it. If necessary, it might be wise to use a short rope here for the security of less experienced walkers.

The Pic de Viscos. The final pull to its summit cross is steep and friable in places.

Approaching Col de Riou on the ascent of Pic de Viscos. In the background are the popular winter hills north of the Barèges valley.

Lower down a neat col is reached followed by a dramatic and steep ascent to the top of Viscos, a confined space topped by a large iron cross.

The return journey also requires caution until the easier ground of the Tuc des Arribans is reached. And on the way back, why not tackle all those minor tops?

From the Col de Riou a narrow path descends due south to a couple of small (and often dried up) lakes, and from here an alternative line of descent may be made following the ski tows.

Ascent: (Col de Riou) 1h: Descent: 0h 45
Ascent: (Soum des Aulhères) 0h 30: Descent: 0h 30
Ascent: (Pic de Viscos) 1h 15: Descent: 1h

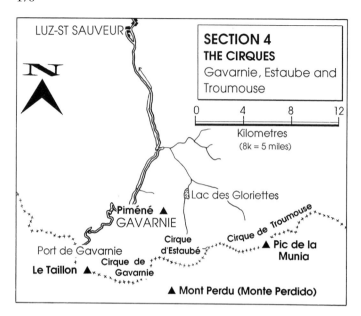

LUZ-ST SAUVEUR

N

SECTION 4
THE CIRQUES
Gavarnie, Estaube and
Troumouse

0   4   8   12

Kilometres
(8k = 5 miles)

Lac des Gloriettes

▲ Piméné ▲
GAVARNIE

Cirque de Troumouse

Cirque
d'Estaubé   ▲ Pic de la
Munia

Port de Gavarnie

Le Taillon ▲   Cirque de
Gavarnie

▲ Mont Perdu (Monte Perdido)

SECTION 4: THE CIRQUES: GAVARNIE, ESTAUBE AND TROUMOUSE

Walk 68 Pic Entre-les-Ports (2476m: 8123ft) Grade C 'Port' is a Pyrenean term for a col, but with the added specific meaning of a place that has been a crossing point for people over the centuries. The two 'ports' that this minor but prominent peak lies between are the Port de Gavarnie (Col de Boucharo) and the Port Vieux (Col des Espécières). The former lies at the head of the vallée de Pouey Aspé, reached by the long and winding road ascending from Gavarnie initially through the vallée des Espécières. The latter further north and less obvious, lies at the head of the vallée des Espécières. As a result of this configuration, the Pic Entre-les-Ports enjoys a unique position with a splendid view, and is well worth the modest amount of time taken to reach its double-topped summit.

Begin from the Col de Tentes, where the winding road from

From the Port de Gavarnie (Col de Boucharo) the view down into Spain and its distant mountains is quite breathtaking.

Pic Entre les Ports.

Gavarnie crosses from the vallée des Espécières to the vallée de Pouey Aspé. There is ample room to park a car. Ascend the grassy ridge running southwest. The going underfoot is in places uneven, and strong footwear advisable.

The ridge brings you directly to the northern, and lower summit from where the higher top, overlooking the Col de Boucharo may easily be reached.
Ascent: 1h: Descent: 0h 45

The whole of this region is remarkable for its birdlife. Vultures are frequently seen overhead, and eagles, too, while the cries of alpine choughs may be heard all day long, mingling with the less strident calls of wheatears, alpine accentors, rock buntings, alpine swifts, black redstarts, rock martins and the like.

Walk 69 Pic de Tentes (2322m: 7618ft) and Lac des Espécières (2195m: 7201ft) Grade C/D These are two easy walks attainable from the Col de Tentes.

69a Pic de Tentes This modest elevation is an excellent coign of vantage for the whole wall of rock and ice extending from the peaks of Les Gabiétous to the Brèche de Roland, and is well worth the short stroll on that account alone.

From the parking spot at the Col de Tentes follow an easy path running northeast over a succession of minor bumps and hollows to the summit, situated on the very boundary of the National Park. In summer the path, like every other path in the Pyrenees is alive with the sounds and sight of thousands, perhaps even millions of crickets that spring from your feet at every step.

Ascent: 0h 30: Descent: 0h 30

69b Lac des Espécières From the Col de Tentes a good path runs easily to the lakes, a spot popular with visitors, lying directly beneath the Col des Espécières. The best time for this short walk is out of the main holiday season, when, especially early in the day or late afternoon, you can have the lakes to yourself.

Time: 1h

In spring, when motorised progress is restricted by snow lying across the roadway, a trek to the lakes from the highest point attainable by car is a pleasant and easy undertaking.

Walk 70 Pic Mourgat (2101m: 6893ft) Grade C The Pic Mourgat is a minor top southwest of Gavarnie, but it offers an unrivalled view of the immense Cirque de Gavarnie. Its ascent should trouble no one, especially if made from the ski station (Les Espécières).

70a From Gavarnie As you enter the centre of Gavarnie a one-way traffic system forces you into an intimate acquaintance with the various beasts of burden that convey tourists to the famous Cascade du Gavarnie. During the height of the season it

Astazou, and the Marboré massif from the ascent of Pic Mourgat.

is difficult to avoid these or the messages of goodwill they leave behind, wherever you park. The best parking will be found along the road opposite La Ruade bar-restaurant.

Walk into Gavarnie and take the minor road (to the right as you enter the main thoroughfare) leading to the church and the cemetery. This precedes a good path (eventually climbing to the Plateau de Bellevue), but after only a short distance double back on a path heading north-northwest towards the road to the Col de Boucharo (Port de Gavarnie). This is a long-established footpath leading to the Granges de Holle (a Club Alpin Français hut), and it avoids much of the trek along the road, with its many circuitous hairpins. The maps show a confusing array of footpaths, but fortunately the route is not difficult to follow on the ground, heading for the Torrent de Holle which it then follows as far as the Cascade du Terrail.

From the waterfalls of Terrail ascend a path towards the east for a while, then climbing in zigzags to the spot height 1844, where such path as there was becomes grassed over, climbing, steeply in places, to the summit, now prominent ahead. As you near the top a small escarpment forms on the left, and a path reappears uncertainly to steer you to the summit and its immense view.

Ascent: 2h 30: Descent: 1h 30

70b From Les Espécières From the parking area around the ski station, which in summer has a rather ghostly look about it, the start of the path for Pic Mourgat is evident enough, leaving the south side of the road not far from the ski station buildings. With only modest ascent it leads to the spot height 1844, where the above route is joined.

Ascent: 1h: Descent: 0h 45

Walk 71 Refuge de la Brèche de Roland from Gavarnie (2587m: 8487ft) Grade B/C Nowhere could be better designed to inspire

Le Taillon and Les Gabiétous from the Col de Tentes.

the hearts and minds of mountain-going mortals than the Refuge de la Brèche de Roland, also known as the Refuge des Sarradets. Poised, precariously it seems, beneath the great walls of the Cirque de Gavarnie and with a grandstand view of the Brèche de Roland, the Casque, the Pic du Marboré and the Grande Cascade de Gavarnie, the Refuge is, not surprisingly, nearly always full.

The easiest ascent to the Refuge is from the Port de Gavarnie (Col de Boucharo), but fit walkers will enjoy the ascent from Gavarnie, leaving behind the equine contributions to road surfacing that testify to the immense popularity of this enclave with visitors from all over the world.

There are two equally pleasant ascents to the Refuge, though one, via the Échelle des Sarradets, is significantly more demanding than the other, via the Bellevue plateau. There is a lot to be said for ascending by the former and descending by the latter, but don't expect a relaxed day.

71a The Échelle des Sarradets Of the three possible ascents, this approach is the longest, but it is also the most beautiful, and the most dramatic. No place for complete novices, this is the most difficult and at times there is an intimidating air about it.

The approach leaves Gavarnie at the end of the main street and follows the left bank of the river as far as Pont de Nadau where it crosses to the right bank. The path is one of many maintained by the National Park and leads to a large plateau, La Prade Saint-Jean, before climbing through forest to the Hôtellerie du Cirque. From the hotel a path continues towards the great waterfall, and you should follow this for a short distance (about 200m) until you can leave it by crossing right, over a small bridge. A path, more or less waymarked, then climbs towards the southwest, heading for the great walls of the cirque.

Eventually you find yourself in a slight depression to the right of some waterfalls, and marked by a small grassy cone-shaped hillock on which a path climbs in a series of zigzags. Even to the experienced eye it is sometimes difficult to figure out quite where the correct onward line of ascent lies as you find yourself at the foot of the Échelle des Sarradets, but from the hollow look for a vague ledge climbing roughly in a northerly direction. This, the 'ladder' in fact, can be climbed easily enough by means of numerous little rock ledges and conveniently projecting rocks, though the prospect may seem a little daunting. Daubs of paint on the rocks keep you on the right line, and after several minor rocksteps the path turns sharply to the south and starts to cross a series of small rocky terraces before reaching a short horizontal stretch. One more zig to the north and a zag to the south and you arrive on the grassy slopes

All that remains of the once massive Glacier du Taillon. Le Doigt (left) and the slopes leading to the summit.

of the vallon des Sarradets, finally above the first of the great rocky terraces that characterise the cirque.

Now the path continues southwest to cross to the true right of the valley at the foot of a series of rocky ridges. From there it climbs in short zigzags along the line of the valley, on steeply sloping mountain pastureland.

Eventually (it seems like a lifetime), the angle of ascent relaxes, the grass, such as it is, gives way to stones and boulders, while still ahead lies the Col des Sarradets. According to the conditions, a direct line may be taken for the Refuge once it comes into view, though the scree is of the worst kind. In many ways it is better to make for the Col itself, and to turn around there to follow the better, but in some conditions still precarious, descending path to the Refuge. About four hours basking in the sun should have you ready to set off back down. Ascent: 4h-5h: Descent: 3h 30

71b The Plateau de Bellevue This is the former classic ascent and the more frequently used before the new route was constructed from the Col de Boucharo. It is rather longer than the Col de Boucharo route, but it is more varied and holds greater interest. Situated on the west flank of the valley, the plateau is a fine vantage point, and many visitors to Gavarnie are content to wander only this far before returning.

As you enter the main street of Gavarnie (a clockwise one-way system) turn immediately right and take a narrow side road leading to the church and the cemetery. The route crosses the lower slopes of Pic Mourgat, keeping to the edge of woodland before two series of zigzags (the Entortes de Bellevue) lead easily to the plateau itself.

On reaching the plateau keep right when a path descends left to Prade Saint-Jean and continue west-southwest into the vallée de Pouey-Aspé. For a while the path is level or rising slightly, but at spot height 1873 the path for the Refuge branches left, and some real effort is called for. First the path descends slightly to cross the Gave des Tourettes and then zigzags its way through the first major rock terrace. A wide sweep to the east takes you across the stream issuing from the Glacier du Taillon, before the path, quite a popular thoroughfare in summer, climbs again through glacial debris to join the route from the Col de Boucharo with which it shares the remaining stretch across the Col des Sarradets and down slightly to the refuge.

Ascent: 3h 30-4h: Descent: 2h 45

Walk 72 Le Taillon (3144m: 10,315ft) Grade B In spite of being the easiest of the Pyrenean 3000m summits to ascend, Le Taillon is nevertheless a mountain demanding all the customary precautions, and if from a distance you can see snow beneath the Brèche de Roland it would be wise to carry an ice-axe. Properly equipped, you will experience in return a

Looking northwest to the Vignemale massif from the ascent of Le Taillon.

The Brèche de Roland from its refuge. In summer the route follows the shaly ridge left of centre.

rewarding and exhilarating ascent, with few difficulties, and much to encourage you to explore these mountains further.

The ascent begins from the Col de Boucharo (Port de Gavarnie) (2270m), on the frontier with Spain. There is limited parking here, and an early start is needed in order to find a spot. But in summer it is not unusual to find a long line of cars extending down the road almost as far as the Col de Tentes.

From the car parking follow a good path (HRP) running south of east. The greater part of this section is almost horizontal, and leads to the foot of the Glacier du Taillon. Here you need both to negotiate the streams issuing from the glacier and the polished rocks rendered smooth by its action. The glacier is now much diminished, and barely touches the route, but snow often lingers here well into July, calling for a certain amount of caution. If snow is absent, the route presents no difficulty, except in the form of the cascades spilling from the glacier above, and these merely threaten a chilly soaking. Cross the stream, ascending in zigzags to the Col des Sarradets (2589m) where the Refuge de la Brèche suddenly and dramatically springs into view.

The next short section to the Refuge is perhaps the most dangerous, especially if you encounter hard snow underfoot, as is often the case. The risk of a slip should not be under-estimated.

Once at the Refuge the whole panorama of the Cirque de Gavarnie opens up magnificently. The highest summit in view is the Pic du Marboré, while nearer to hand, and prominent on the skyline, is the Brèche de Roland, a feature with an unjustified place in French legend. Roland, nephew of Charlemagne, commanded Charlemagnes rearguard on its withdrawal from Spain on 15 August 778. According to an ancient poem, the *Song of Roland*, the rearguard was attacked by Saracens, and when all was lost Roland, mortally wounded, tried to break his magical sword, Durandal, by striking it on a

Pico Blanco, a Spanish mountain, from below the Brèche de Roland.

rock. The sword remained unbroken, but the rock was split asunder, providing what today is the Brèche de Roland. All historical accounts of the action however record that the withdrawal in fact occurred a hundred kilometres west of Gavarnie, at Roncevaux.

This has not stopped the Brèche becoming a place of romantic tourism over the centuries. In 1828 the Duchesse de Berry, widow of the assassinated second son of Charles X, ascended to it from Gavarnie, carried up in a chair. Juliette Drouet, mistress of Victor Hugo, was most put out that a woman other than herself should have accomplished this feat, and claimed that the Duchesse needed thirty porters; less jaundiced opinions mention only two. Either way, the Duchesse arrived back at Gavarnie 'still merry and confident'; no mention however is made of the condition of the porters!

The continuation to the Brèche is quite clear, and ascends a

Le Doigt: the domed summit of Le Taillon lies beyond, and the route passes through the Fausse Brèche to the right of Le Doigt.

Walkers at the Brèche de Roland.

Pic des Sarradets from the Brèche de Roland. You can judge the scale from the walkers left of the patch of snow.

moderate slope, usually covered with snow and often with stretches of ice; in these conditions an ice-axe is needed and crampons may be essential. With a view to returning this way (over which you have little choice) it would be wise to observe the way rocks dislodged by walkers nearing the Brèche find their way down the small permanent snow field, and plan your descent accordingly.

As you pass through the Brèche (2807m) it is a revelation to see how thin the apparently substantial wall of rock really is. The gap is no more than 40m wide and about 100m high, and caused by the collapse of the wall. Once into Spain it is the great contrast between the two landscapes which is remarkable: on the one hand a rugged landscape of snow, ice, forests and savage rocks, on the other a softer, gentler, more barren scene of sun-scorched sierras and valleys. Just on the Spanish side of the frontier in 1926 one of the great speleologists of the

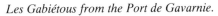

Les Gabiétous from the Port de Gavarnie.

Le Casque (upper right of picture) and the Marboré complex.

Pyrenees, Norbert Casteret, discovered an underground glacier, the highest ice-cavern known.

Continue through the gap and turn right (west) on a path running beneath the towering walls of Le Bazillac (beware occasional stone- or ice-falls) until it abruptly ends at La Fausse Brèche. A short way on a curious pillar of rock, Le Doigt, is passed on the north, and so back in to France. The rock here is more friable and, if covered with snow and ice, the short stretch around Le Doigt is potentially dangerous. Once around however it is a simple pull to Le Taillon, from where the view to the east takes in Marboré, Mont Perdu, and Cilindro. Vignemale is prominent to the north-west.
Ascent: 3h: Descent: 2h

Walk 73 Les Gabiétous (3034m: 9954ft) Grade B This double-topped summit rises directly above the Col de Boucharo (2270m), from where a direct ascent by its glacier or its north face can be made by experienced climbers, but not by walkers. However Les Gabiétous can be added to the ascent of Le

Taillon, and will provide a peaceful and seldom visited extension for walkers with time to spare.

Follow Walk 72 to the summit of Le Taillon and from there descend the frontier crest towards the southwest, and then west towards the Col des Gabiétous (2935m). On the descent to the Col the rocks change colour, becoming greyish. At a cairn take a distinct path, on the right, which passes beneath a short steep section to rejoin the crest at Le Taillons west peak, beyond which an easy descent takes you to the Col.

The Col des Gabiétous is divided by a small pinnacle which can be tackled in two ways. Either climb the pinnacle, descending a little on the Spanish side: this is not difficult, but care is needed and there is a sense of exposure. Alternatively, a longer but more reassuring route turns the pinnacle on the Spanish side, and then scrambles easily back to the crest and the first summit, Le Gabiétous oriental (3031m).

The continuation to the second and higher summit, Le Gabitou occidental, follows the ridge to the southwest. At

Le Casque: the route passes below the cliffs to the prominent col.

times it is an airy traverse, but it is easy and any problems can be avoided on the Spanish side.

Ascent: 4h 30: Descent: 3h 30

Walkers wanting to avoid reversing too much of their outward route can develop a circular tour of these summits from the Brèche de Roland.

The key to this round is the appropriately named Pic Blanc (Pico Blanco: 2923m) lying west-southwest from the Brèche. Nearer to hand is a rocky hollow containing a number of small lakes, and your route goes through this hollow. Continue from the Brèche on the path for Le Taillon for about 50m and then descend gradually into the hollow. The going is very difficult underfoot, and it is better to keep descending rather than to try to retain height.

Once past the lakes (keep them to your left) you encounter a glacial moraine and then a short ochre-coloured ridge due south of Le Doigt. Ascend this ridge until you regain the level of the Brèche de Roland, and then head southwest to the obvious col to the north of Pic Blanc (2840m), from which that summit may be easily reached.

Descend a little from the Col towards the northwest and then traverse horizontally into the valley to the south of the Col des Gabiétous. At about 2870m, lower down than the col, climb to the left (west) and head towards the crest between the two summits. An easy walk takes you first to the higher summit, occidental, from where you can reverse the route described above to the summit of Le Taillon. This variant is by no means difficult, but it is tiring, and the temptation to descend direct to the Col de Boucharo should be strongly resisted. As a result this circuit is very demanding on time and energy.

Walk 74 Le Casque (3000m: 9842ft) Grade B Towering impressively just to the southeast of the Brèche de Roland, Le

Pic du Marboré, and the upper Grande Cascade.

Casque, like Le Taillon, is a relatively easy 3000m summit to achieve. But it would be irresponsible to suggest that even these 'easy' summits do not have their darker aspects. Walkers should therefore be properly equipped, and at certain times of the year, that means carrying ice-axes and crampons for security, the things you need most when you have forgotten to bring them.

The greater part of the ascent, as far as the Brèche de Roland corresponds with that for the ascent of Le Taillon (Walk 72). Having reached the Brèche it is well worth a few minutes studying the way ahead to avoid losing too much height or wandering off into the valleys of Spain.

Descend from the Brèche towards the southeast, traversing along the base of limestone cliffs on a route that is either a grey and dusty trail across stones or snow slopes, according to the time of year. After about fifteen to twenty minutes, and having lost in the region of 90m (300ft) of height, you start climbing again to cross a narrow ledge (equipped with a cable for security) called the Pas des Isards. Another ten minutes or so and you have the Col des Isards below you on the right.

The path descends slightly for a few minutes before climbing again towards the northeast. Shortly you discover a large hollow lying between the Casque (which is now to the northwest) and La Tour (to the northeast), through which a cairned path sets off (left) northwest.

This stretch of the frontier is renowned for numerous spectacular ice caves, though they should only be entered by experienced people, and shortly you will encounter the entrance to one of them, at about 2850m. Soon after the cave the path continues towards the west and reaches the crest descending southwards from the summit of the Casque. In spite of having steep drops on your left and a few places where the use of hands becomes obligatory, the ascent of this crest is quite easy and leads you directly to the summit, a quite stunning viewpoint.

Ascent: 3h 30: Descent: 2h 30

Walk 75 La Tour (3009m: 9872ft) Grade B La Tour is but a minor bump along the top of the great Cirque de Gavarnie, but a suitable excursion for a day, especially for walkers based at the Refuge de la Brèche de Roland; it will certainly be less populated than its neighbours and its chief fame rests on the exploits of rock and winter climbers on its north face.

The route shares that for the ascent of Le Casque (Walk 74) as far as the open hollow between Le Casque and La Tour, where, instead of making your way upwards, you continue along a path to a wide shelf crossing the southern slopes of La Tour. Soon a chimney, marked by a cairn, is reached on the left and, though frequently blocked by snow, it may be climbed without difficulty by its left wall until it opens on to an upper terrace, rather like the one you have just left.

Turn right along this terrace, and then ascend left to the edge of the Cirque de Gavarnie, reaching it about one kilometre east

The Vallée de Pouey Aspé.

of La Tour, where a spectacular view awaits. Now move west along the edge, rising steadily by easy slopes to a point a little south of the summit, from where an easy ascent may be made to the highest point.

Ascent: (From Col de Boucharo): 4h: Descent: 3h
Ascent: (From Refuge de la Brèche de Roland): 2h 45:
Descent: 1h 45

Walk 76 Pic du Marboré (3248m: 10,656ft) Grade B Presenting to the north a figure befitting its status as the highest of the summits along the Cirque de Gavarnie, the Pic du Marboré is just a little let down by its posterior, a broad, sun-scorched flank by means of which a comparatively easy ascent may be made. Even so, the route is a long one, and given the power of the noonday sun, best tackled early in the morning from an

La Tour, Le Casque and the Refuge de la Brèche de Roland, from the Col des Sarradets.

overnight stay at the Refuge de la Brèche de Roland.

From the Refuge, follow Walk 75 for La Tour, climbing the chimney to reach the upper terrace, and continuing east to the edge of the upper wall of the Cirque de Gavarnie about one kilometre east of La Tour where the two routes now separate.

Continue east along the top of the cirque to reach the Col de la Cascade (2931m: 9616ft) where there is a breathtaking view into the Cirque, of the great summit of Cilindro further east, and Monte Perdido (Mont Perdu) southeast. The path is marked by small cairns and continues east, leaving the edge of the cirque and rising to top the 3000m mark as it makes for the southwest ridge of Cilindro. About halfway between the Col de la Cascade and the southwest ridge of Cilindro you need to leave the path and climb for just over a kilometre by easy boulder slopes, often snow-covered, slightly east of north, later heading north-northwest up the barren southern slopes of Pic du Marboré.

Ascent: (From Refuge de la Brèche de Roland) 3h 30-4h: Descent: 2h 45

Ascent: (From Col de Boucharo) 5h-6h: Descent: 4h

Walk 77 Piméné (2801m: 9190ft) Grade B/C With some justification, Piméné is considered to be one of the finest vantage points in this region of the Pyrenees. Not in itself an unduly difficult mountain to climb, though it is quite steep in places, nor especially interesting, the arrival at its summit on a clear day is a satisfying achievement.

The best time of year for Piméné is July or September when you generally avoid the remnant clouds of yesterday's afternoon storms that add an interesting dimension to ascents earlier in the year, and also the worst of the August heat. Even so, and an early start is important if you want to reach the coolness of altitude before melting point.

Piméné.

Leave Gavarnie by the track at the southern end of the main street and follow this to Pont Brioule. Cross the bridge and continue for about 500m until, where the usually dry gully of the Alans stream reaches the valley, you can take a National Park footpath climbing towards the east, and later, by a steep series of zigzags, to the southeast. This path climbs without difficulty to the pleasant mountain pastures of the Plateau de Pailla and its cabin at 1800m.

From the cabin the path now sweeps northwards and back southeast, taking the sting out of the ascent and eventually reaching the National Park's Refuge des Espuguettes. There is a fine view here of the two Astazou peaks to the south, while Piméné lies some distance to the northeast.

From the hut the path continues eastwards towards the long southern ridge of the mountain, until, just on the 2260m contour, it reaches a fork. Now the path (left branch) heads north-northwest before climbing steeply by a series of zigzags to the Col de Piméné (2522m). To the north rises the minor top of the Petit Piméné, but at the Col cross to the eastern side of this point above the Estaube valley, eventually to regain the crest over rocks northeast of the Petit Piméné at 2647m. A steady and steep pull now leads to the main summit from which, unseen from the Gavarnie valley, there is a view of Monte Perdido (Mont Perdu).

Ascent: (From Gavarnie) 4h 30-5h: Descent: 3h

Ascent: (From Refuge des Espuguettes) 2h 30: Descent: 1h 30

Walk 78 La Grande Cascade Grade C This waterfall is the highest in Europe, spouting water more than 420m (nearly 1400ft) from a hidden terrace and glacier in the southeastern corner of the Cirque de Gavarnie. The true magnitude of the Cascade, and for that matter the Cirque itself, are not readily apparent from the village. The sheer enormity of the walls, greater even than the North Face of the Grandes Jorasses in the Alps above Chamonix, can only be appreciated by making the trip with everyone else to the Col de la Cascade, the lowest point along the crest of the Cirque. The height difference from the base of the Cirque is almost 1350m (4420ft); to the summit of Pic du Marboré it is 1664m (5460ft).

The route to the Grande Cascade is not in its early stages difficult to follow, and might well be called The Manure Trail. Thankfully, the weary trains of horses, donkeys and mules only go as far as the Hôtellerie du Cirque, leaving walkers with the final approach to the scree slopes at the foot of the Cascade rather more to themselves.

Leave Gavarnie at the southern end of the main street and follow the left bank of the river as far as the Pont de Nadau, where you cross to the right bank. From here the National Park authority has carried out much needed pathway improvement where it crosses a large plateau, La Prade Saint Jean. Shortly, the path climbs among the trees of the Bois d'Arribama and continues easily to the hotel, an idyllic setting for a hotel though it no longer offers accommodation.

Onwards the path continues towards the Cascade, leaving behind a majority of the visitors. At one point it is necessary to ford the Torrent d'Astazou-Barrade, though it can often be crossed by a snow bridge. As you ascend, now in the barren and rocky amphitheatre at the very heart of the Cirque de Gavarnie, the path becomes less clear, but the objective remains obvious enough, and it is not long before you are negotiating bouldery ground to gain the fan of scree below the falls, and a thorough drenching from spray.

There have been proposals, thankfully consigned to oblivion, to construct a dam just above Gavarnie with the intention of reforming a lake that existed here many years ago, held in place by a plug of glacial moraine before a landslide opened the way to the valley. And while the notion of winter skating or of a waterfall plunging directly into sky-blue waters has a certain romantic appeal, the thought of what the entrepreneurs would make of it is too horrifying a prospect for words.

Ascent: 2h: Descent: 1h 45

Walk 79 Estaubé valley and Cirque d'Estaubé: Port Neuf de Pinède (2466m: 8090ft) Grade C Immediately east of Gavarnie lie two more enchanting valleys headed by enormous cirques of rock, Estaubé and Troumouse, with the added attraction of a quiet retreat far from the thronging streets of Gavarnie.

The first of these valleys, Estaubé, provides an uncomplicated walk well into its upper reaches before the skills and judgements of experienced walkers are called for. At its northern end a dam, designed for electricity generation, now impounds the tumultuous streams pouring from the mountainsides in the Lac des Gloriettes, while to the south a crenellated ridge of summits gives way to the greater height of Mont Perdu (Monte Perdido) beyond. Two passes link the valley with Spain: the first, the Brèche de Tuquerouye, finds room for a small refuge, the oldest French Alpine Club hut in the Pyrenees, built in 1890, still very basic, but combining limited accommodation with a most dramatic setting. One of the early pioneers of Pyrenean mountaineering, Baron Louis-François Ramond de Carbonnières (1755-1827), crossed into Spain by the Brèche de Tuquerouye in 1797 on his attempt to scale Mont Perdu. Of the valley he wrote: 'Nothing spoils the design both severe and bold; and the colour, too, so transparent and pure – it is grey a little warmed with pink – suits equally the light or shade, and softens the contrast between them . . .'

The second pass, the Port Neuf de Pinède, is an old smugglers' pass, and a long established route of pilgrimage through the mountains. Walk 79 describes the way to this ancient crossing point, but such is the charm of the valley, and so relaxing its air, that one's arrival at the pass may come rather more by accident than by design. Along much of the walk the way is decorated in summer by beautiful stands of iris, vivid purple-blue against the more subdued colours of the valley.

Entering the Estaubé valley, with the Cirque d'Estaubé beyond.

Lac des Gloriettes.

The Gloriettes dam is approached along a minor road (signposted 'Héas') leaving the N21 after the second hairpin bend south of Gèdre. Leave this minor road to cross the Pont de l'Arraillé and ascend the serpentine road that follows to the dam. There is plenty of room to park near the dam and, crossing this, you reach a path circling around the western flank of the lake. At the southern end a wide grassy plateau is reached just above a few small falls. Deeper into the valley the path passes through a narrow gorge before opening out once more near the Cabane d'Estaubé. The quality of the pasturage in this highland setting is so sought after that over 2000 sheep are pastured here during the summer months. High above, circling around the head of the valley east to west, rise the Pic d'Estaubé, the Pic Blanc, Port Neuf de Pinède, followed by the long crest that stretches to the Grand Astazou, notched by the Brèche de Tuquerouye, and finally Pic Rouge de Pailla perched above the Hourquette d'Alans, by which route a crossing may be made directly to Gavarnie.

For those bound for the Port Neuf de Pinède some uphill

work is needed as you climb in zigzags to a meeting of pathways just below Pic Rouge de Pailla. If you go right here you eventually reach the Hourquette d'Alans, while left you climb a little more before gaining a rather easier traverse to the final pull to the pass.

Marmots are frequently found lower down the valley, but among the rocks and boulders of the higher ground it is ptarmigan and the occasional stoat that you should look for. Griffon vultures and golden eagles are frequently seen overhead, while a variety of smaller birds, black redstart, alpine accentor, wheatear and Alpine chough are invariable companions throughout the whole of the walk. En route, as the path traverses below the crest, you will pass the pyramidal shape of the Borne de Tuquerouye which marks the entrance to the precarious couloir ascending to the Brèche de Tuquerouye, and quite out of bounds for inexperienced walkers.

Ascent: (To Port de Pinède) 5h: Descent: 3h 45

Walk 80 Cirque de Troumouse (2133m: 6998ft) Grade C East of the Cirque d'Estaubé lies the largest true cirque in the Pyrenees, the Cirque de Troumouse, a massive four kilometres in diameter, and a vast amphitheatre contained by three-quarters of a circle of almost level headwall. Like the Estaubé valley, Troumouse is largely unspoiled, very much the secluded preserve of the mountain walker.

The key to the walk is the hamlet of Héas, reached by a minor road from Gèdre. In due course you encounter the turning (right) leading to the Gloriettes dam and the Cirque d'Estaubé. Pass this by and continue along the road to Héas. Along the southern flank of the road is the massive side of a mountain called Poueyboucou part of which collapsed in 1650 following three days of torrential rain, damming the valley and causing a lake to form that extended up the valley beyond the Chapelle de Héas, submerging everything. So it remained for almost 140 years until, in September 1788, more violent storms swept aside the debris that had plugged the valley. These days there is little evidence of the disaster, and the Gave de Héas now meanders in all innocence across the once flooded plateau.

Beyond the chapel at Héas the road into the valley becomes a toll road and climbs 580m (1900ft) higher into the cirque with about as much sense of purpose as a snail with terminal wanderlust. If the experience of being among the mountains is all you seek, there is much to be said for having someone drive you up the serpentine toll road, from the end of which you can walk the short and comparatively easy distance to the Lacs des Aires.

Walk 80 however begins lower down, not far from the Chapel, which is worth a visit. Legend has it that during its construction wild goats would suddenly appear each morning, allowing the three masons engaged on the job to have fresh milk each day.

Just by the toll (*péage*) a path sets off on a direct route for the Cabane des Aires, but after only 150m leave this for a National Park path ascending northeast, at first easily and then in zigzags, into the vallon de l'Aguila. Remain on the left bank of the stream throughout the ascent, which brings you first to the Cabane de l'Aguila on the opposite bank, and almost immediately to the Oratoire de la Sainte Famille. There is a tale, dating to the 15th century, that one day the shepherds of Héas saw three white doves flying across the summits of the Aguila. The first of these alighted on the edge of the hanging valley where the oratory stands today; the second descended into the main valley to alight on the spot now occupied by the Chapel of Héas, while the third finally came to rest on a small hillock overlooking the vallée d'Azun, where you will find the Chapel of Pouey-Laun.

Southeast of the oratory it is possible to gain a rising slope beneath the crest that ultimately leads to the Pic de Gerbats. A path, sometimes waymarked, but otherwise betraying its popularity with winter skiers, sets off towards the Cabane des Aires, squeezing awkwardly through the gap between the Tour de Lieusaube and the steep cliffs to the west of it, and where the angle of ascent eases as it contours to the cabin and on to the Lacs des Aires. An inscription outside the Cabane des Aires, written in one of the dialects of the region ('U toy non cragn que Diu et péricle et era lit'), provides a clue to the philosophy of the mountain shepherds, telling that they fear only God, thunder and avalanches, the latter a possible reference to the 1650 disaster. There is always danger in these high mountains, but for the people who eke a living from them, it is the invisible forces and natural phenomena that constitute the greatest threat.

Between the Cabane and the lakes a gentle path leads on through boulder slopes, scree and grassy patches. Looking south, the great limestone wall of the cirque is a forbidding prospect, riven by gullies, still holding remnant patches of snow and ice, echoing to the call of Alpine choughs and the staccato call of black redstarts; a place to make the spine tingle, and the heart miss a beat. Highest of the summits along the cirque is the Pic de la Munia, prominent to the southeast, and to the north of which stand two vertical pinnacles, the Two Sisters of Troumouse.

The Lacs des Aires, lying in the very heart of this vast ring of mountains, are a collection of misshapen ponds around which the path skirts to begin a gentle climb and descent to the roadhead.

Walkers without transport and so having to descend the road to Héas should follow the road faithfully at least until beyond Le Maillet, and only then consider taking advantage of shortcuts.

Time: 5h

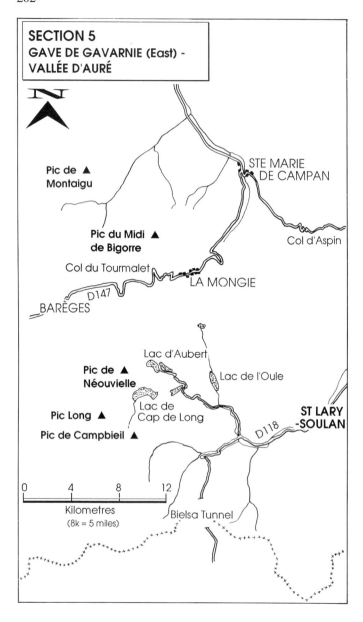

SECTION 5
GAVE DE GAVARNIE (East) -
VALLÉE D'AURÉ

N

Pic de ▲
Montaigu

STE MARIE
DE CAMPAN

Pic du Midi ▲
de Bigorre

Col d'Aspin

Col du Tourmalet

LA MONGIE

D147

BARÈGES

Lac d'Aubert

Pic de ▲
Néouvielle

Lac de l'Oule

Pic Long ▲

Lac de
Cap de Long

ST LARY
-SOULAN

D118

Pic de Campbieil ▲

0   4   8   12

Kilometres
(8k = 5 miles)

Bielsa Tunnel

SECTION 5: GAVE DE GAVARNIE (EAST) TO VALLÉE D'AURÉ

Walk 81 Pic de Nerbiou (1747m: 5732ft) Grade C The collection of summits north of the Barèges valley are of more modest elevation than those closer to the frontier, and, except in winter, receive much less attention as a result. Nevertheless, they are not to be underestimated, and offer a splendid selection of walks that serve as a taster for excursions into the higher and more inaccessible corners of the Pyrenees.

The Pic de Nerbiou rises to the east of the semi-industrial complex of Pierrefitte-Nestalas-Soulom. Anyone ascending first to the winter ski station of Hautacam can virtually wander up Nerbiou at will, following the ridge from the col just west of Pic de Moulata.

Rather more demanding is a route from the tiny village of Ortiac, reached from Soulom, along the D13 to Villelongue and then by the serpentine road to the village.

From the roadside cross in the village head left (north) along a waymarked route that becomes narrow and lined with hedges. Soon, as it approaches the Isaby stream, the path widens again and leads to a bridge beyond which it zigzags fairly steeply northeast into woodland. At a fork go right (east) and continue to the ruins of the Abbaye de St. Orens. Pass to the left of the ruins and continue to another fork. Go left this time (north) and press on to a sharp bend at 975m. Continue following the path, climbing easily on leaving the wood.

As the gradient eases leave the path and ascend north, aiming for a low supporting wall that retains a man-made watercourse. Follow this northwest for about one and a half kilometres towards a large reservoir, but leave the path slightly before reaching the reservoir for a steeper path climbing north and then northeast to reach more ruins at the Plaa d'Arribaut (1180m). Now more or less follow the ridge, passing the top of a dry ravine, the entrance to an abandoned mine and its service road. Cross the road and climb the shallow valley beyond, aiming north to reach the end of the west-northwest ridge of Nerbiou, and follow the upper limits of the Bois de Mailh Blanc to within striking distance of the summit.

Ascent: 3h: Descent: 2h 15

Walk 82 Soum de Nère (2394m: 7854ft) Grade B/C The Soum de Nère lies concealed high among the folds of the mountains northeast of Luz-St Sauveur, visible only from adjoining ranges. As a result it is not often visited. The ascent, certainly from the mountain village of Sers, is frequently steep, but the reward is one of the finest views of the Cirque de Gavarnie and Mont Perdu.

About two kilometres below Barèges a narrow road leads to Sers, one of a number of tiny communities clinging to the hillsides in this most attractive region of the Pyrenees.

From Sers pass in front of the war memorial and the bar/restaurant and, just after the school, climb a gravel and cement track leading to the highest part of the village. Then locate a good path zigzagging northwards as far as the barns at Boussie from where it continues up slightly easier slopes, at least as far as some higher barns at 1486m. Now look for an isolated tree about 200m away (north-northwest) and yet further away (600m) a collapsed barn near two trees. A long-established footpath passes between these two points, and from the ruined barn climbs a grassy spur, heading northwest.

Once on the spur use paths ascending obliquely towards the north, taking care to avoid other and more tempting paths heading northeast, which ultimately contribute nothing to the walk other than unnecessary effort.

On a grassy plateau to the northeast of Soum d'Espade d'Arbéouse you find the Cabane d'Arbéouse, an excellent landmark from which the path gradually swings round to the

west, climbing comfortably. Due north of Soum d'Espade d'Arbéouse a stream is encountered and this can be followed upwards to a small tarn. From here leave the path and climb grassy slopes to reach the col linking Soum de Nère and Soum d'Espade d'Arbéouse at about 2120m. These slopes are quite steep and casting about from side to side will help ease the angle. Yet even after so much effort, this 'modest' summit still calls for more on the final pull, with significant drops on both sides calling for care, especially if any snow is lingering.
Ascent: 2h 30: Descent: 1h 45

Walk 83 Pic du Midi de Bigorre (2872m: 9422ft) The Pic du Midi de Bigorre possesses one of the most expansive views of all the Pyrenean peaks, and in consequence is probably visited by more people than any other. Though the summit stands well above the snow line, little snow will be found during summer due to the excessively steep sides of the mountain, especially on the north. The date of its first ascent is unknown, but it was regularly ascended by bathers at Bagnères de Bigorre and Barèges before Ramond de Carbonnières walked up it in 1787.

The upper reaches of the Coume du Pic from the Col de Sencours.

Looking northwest from Pic du Midi de Bigorre.

An English lady, Anne Walker, rode to the top on horseback in 1838, and in 1878 an observatory was built almost on the summit. Belloc commented early this century: 'No other of the great mountains of Europe have been put more thoroughly in

Approaching the summit of Pic du Midi de Bigorre.

harness.' Since then the mountain has become even more burdened with the weight of a television mast and more scientific paraphernalia. The top may be reached by cable car from La Mongie, or you can drive up a rough toll road from the Col du Tourmalet, at the end which there is yet another cable car to whisk you to the very top in a matter of minutes.

On days of crystal visibility it is possible to make out the summits of the Massif Central, and on similar nights the lighthouse at Biarritz on the Atlantic coast. The mountain also is the point from which the demarcation between mountain and plain, which characterises the northern slopes of the Pyrenees, becomes very clear. It is worth mentioning, too, that those walkers not averse to spending a night on a mountain to witness both sunset and sunrise, could do worse than choose Pic du Midi de Bigorre.

83a From the Col du Tourmalet Grade C The Col du Tourmalet, at 2115m, is the highest pass in the Pyrenees which you can cross by car; as a result it closes early in the season, usually in November, and can remain closed into June. The name Tourmalet means the 'bad way round', an accolade which the

The upper limits of the toll road leading to the Pic du Midi de Bigorre.

Looking northeast across the Plain of Tarbes from the summit of Pic du Midi de Bigorre.

Col earned in the days before a respectable road was constructed, when you had to hire porters to carry you from one valley to the next.

There is little parking on the Luz-St Sauveur side of the pass, but a convenient space constructed just over the Col. Return to the Col and its attendant hotel and gift shop, beyond which the toll road starts; during the months of July, August and September you will find someone waiting to relieve you of a few francs and hand you a leaflet explaining how badly the road becomes eroded during winter, presumably, as a result of allowing cars to travel up it during summer. Walkers, during these months, should be constantly alert to the dangers of motorists careering up what must be one of the dustiest roads in France: in fact, I would go so far as to recommend avoiding the toll road altogether during these months, while for one day at least in July the D918 itself is taken over as a gruelling mountain stage in the Tour de France cycle race.

The route is obvious, and needs little detailing. Towards the end of the long approach road, at the Col de Sencours, the

ascent from the Val d'Arizes joins, and the way then zigzags, often through massive walls of snow, to the Hôtellerie des Laquets, before the final plod to the summit. It may be unexciting walking, but the view is quite superb.
Ascent: 2h: Descent: 1h 30

83b By the Val d'Arizes Grade B The ascent by the Val d'Arizes was the way taken by scientists en route to the observatory in the days before the road from the Col du Tourmalet. Their porters were invariably so heavily laden they needed a fixed cable above the Col de Sencours to help them on their way.

The ascent begins in Artigues, a little above the Hôtel du Val d'Arizes, by a path along the left bank of a small stream. Follow

▼ *The summit paraphernalia on Pic du Midi de Bigorre. Guided tours are arranged during summer months.*

Looking south to the Néouvielle massif from Pic du Midi de Bigorre. ▼

this for about 50m and then cross the stream. At about 1400m you join the old road to Tourmalet, close by the Cabanes de Tramazaygues. Continue along the left bank of the Arizes which here flows through a deep ravine.

On reaching the Pont des Vaquès cross the stream, and take the path climbing obliquely northwest and then west to the rock step, Passade de Sencours, at the entrance to the Coume de Sencours. The path now ascends northwards, around La Picarde, and into the Coume du Pic, passing on the way the ancient Cabane de Pène Blanque. By way of confusion, the present day Coume de Sencours used to be called the Coume de la Picarde, after the nearby summit, while the Coume du Pic was formerly called the Coume de Sencours . . . No place for a rendezvous on a windswept night if you don't both have the same map!

At the head of the Coume du Pic the path climbs steeply to join the toll road from the Col du Tourmalet at the Col de Sencours, with which it shares the final ascent to the summit. Ascent: 3h: Descent: 2h 30

The upper reaches of the Bastan valley, near the Col du Tourmalet.

Walk 84 Pic de Montaigu (2339m: 7674ft) Grade B/C Seen from the Plain of Tarbes in the north, Montaigu rises so proudly to the right of Pic du Midi de Bigorre that it is often mistaken for one of the great mountains of the Pyrenees. Its summit is still a fine viewpoint, here extending from Pic d'Orhy in the Basque country, across the giants of Balaïtous, Vignemale, Pic Long, and Néouvielle to the summits of Ariège in the east.

About four kilometres (2½ miles) south of Bagnères de Bigorre a minor road leads into the vallée de Lesponne, though the river is the Adour. The road is signposted 'Chiroulet', and when a further signpost indicates that this tiny community is only 3.2 kilometres on, look for and take a motorable forest road on the right. Follow this for about two kilometres through the Bois du Cérétou to a bridge (the third) at 1135m. Beware of descending log-laden lorries, there are few passing places, and even fewer opportunities to park conveniently.

From the bridge climb a sloping forest track on the right bank of the stream, and continue to the Népoutre stream which is crossed just above its confluence with the Tos. The ruins of the Cabane d'Arrolets lie a short way further on, and signal a

The cloud-filled Barèges-Bastan valley. Such cloud formation is commonplace during the summer months, but clear skies await above.

crossing about five minutes later to the left bank of the Tos only to return to the right bank in a further five minutes. Climb a narrow gully from the top of which the Col de Tos is visible. The east face above you is often under snow into July, but lying at an easy angle, and should offer no difficulty in attaining the Col.

From the Col de Tos climb south on a path (one of a number) just on the west side of the ridge. As the gradient eases and the Lacs de Montaigu appear ahead (often under snow and little more than small pools) aim for them, passing to the right, and climb generally west over minor bumps to reach a rocky ridge at col 2091m. Continue now south-southeast on a path near to but just below the ensuing ridge. Cross a small top (2177m) and climb the final ridge to the summit. There are steep drops on either side here and, though the slope is easy, care is needed to guard against a slip on patches of snow.

Ascent: 3h: Descent: 2h

A much longer (in distance) ascent of Montaigu may also be made from the Hautacam ski station virtually following the ridge from the parking area at Moulata. Pass Pic de Naouit on the north (numerous tracks), likewise Pic de Barran and the slightly higher Pic du Mont (though experienced walkers would have no difficulty staying on the ridge), and gain the Col de Barran. The next objective is the Col des Rosques, but a series of rocky ups and downs make the going a bit tedious and time-consuming. The better way is simply to link the two cols across the intervening corrie basin. The ensuing rocky ridge is then followed, with care, to the summit.

Ascent: 3h: Descent: 2h

Walk 85 Lac Bleu (2011m: 6598ft) Grade C Lac Bleu lies beyond the ridge to the north of Barèges, and is appropriately named, for its depth of some 120m and the shelter of the surrounding mountains gives it an intensely rich blueness.

The simplest ascent is from the tiny community of Le Chiroulet in the vallée de Lesponne de l'Adour. From Le Chiroulet a service road climbs into the forest and zigzags mercilessly upwards, leaving the forest and continuing in much the same fashion until it grinds to a halt at a footbridge. The trail however continues zigzagging, across scree and grass until, with much relief, the lake is finally reached (1928m).

Walkers with energy to spare can now follow a rough path all around the lake, with yet a little more climbing to come.

Time: 2 hours to reach the lake; 1h 15 to walk round it, and 1h 45 for the return descent.

Walk 86 Pène det Pourî (2587m: 8487ft) Grade B/C On reaching Lac Bleu (Walk 85) a little more effort will allow you to add the summit due south of the lake, Pène det Pourî to the day's itinerary. It is a fine vantage point.

From the outflow at the northern end of the lake climb northwest across undulating ground, at a distance from and directly above the lake. Cross the small valley leading to the Col de Bareilles and follow the path above the west shore of the lake, climbing a little to cross a spur and then descending once more.

When the path forks (1987m) take the right branch and climb to the Cabane de la Thoue. Just after the cabin enter a small valley ascending west-southwest and climb to a lake, or the remains of a lake at 2217m. The route by this time is no longer on a path, but it is neither difficult to follow nor unduly arduous. From the lake ascend southeast for a while, more or less keeping faith with its feeder stream (usually dry), and roughly heading for the summit, now directly above. The final pull, no more than 30 or 40 metres, is a bit exposed and should be treated with caution.

Ascent: 4h 30: Descent: 3h 15

Walk 87 Pic d'Espade (2467m: 8094ft) Grade B Pic d'Espade is the prominent peak directly above and south of the Col du Tourmalet. The key to its ascent is a track which leaves the ascending D918 about 100m east of the first major hairpin, Tournant des Bernès, a line also used for the ascent of Pic des Quatre Termes (Walk 88). Cars may be parked here, one kilometre above the upper ski station.

The route is common to both ascents only as far as a point due east of the obvious Col du Pic d'Espade, where a small cairn marks the point of departure upwards of a strenuous line through a sea of boulders, with some easing of the difficulties higher up, on the left. Your objective is the Col, which you should not cross, but instead ascend steeply on the east slope of the peak to its summit. This is not one of the most frequently visited summits of the Pyrenees, and walkers may find the energy expended well rewarded by the solitude and airy views, most notably northwards to Pic du Midi de Bigorre.

Ascent: 2h: Descent: 1h 30

Walkers based in La Mongie can make a slightly longer ascent by taking the path from the village centre which runs west, parallel to the Tourmalet road, but south of it. After about 1.5 kilometres this path turns south and climbs in zigzags up to the Coume de Porteilh beneath a cable car line. As the path changes direction leave it and continue south west on a track towards Pic d'Espade, which in due course brings you to the track from the D918.

Ascent: 2h 30: Descent: 2h

Walk 88 Pic des Quatre Termes (2724m: 8937ft) Grade B There is every likelihood that the Pic des Quatre Termes, and its neighbour, Pic d'Espade, are better known to winter visitors on skis than among the walking fraternity. Nearby stands the summer ghost-town of La Mongie with its temporarily redundant ironmongery of winter sports etched starkly against the blue skies of summer. That the region is popular is beyond question, for the town grows by the year as yet more and more hotels and apartments spring up to accommodate the ski-ing hordes. Yet in spite of a backdrop of fine peaks and airy ridges, it is not, unlike Gavarnie or Luz-St Sauveur, a place which commands the attention of walkers.

The Pic des Quatre Termes is, however, a fine vantage point. The approach through Coume de Porteilh presents no route-finding problems, and affords a crossing, via the Pas de la Crabe, into the neighbouring valley of Aygues-Cluses.

From the Tournant des Bernès the broad track initially shared by Walk 87 descends, east of south, but soon rises again, more steeply than it appears, until you reach a point due east of the Col du Pic d'Espade. Here the track descends a little before climbing again, with a low cliff face on your left. Shortly, you reach a lake of crystal clarity on your right, a good place to rest, as you finally enter the Coume de Porteilh, and almost immediately encounter the lower station of the Télésiége des Quatre Termes.

Continue now, more or less following the *télésiège*, and

The dark cliffs of Pic d'Espade lead the eye to Pic des Quatre Termes.

La Mongie, a popular winter ski resort, but something of a forlorn sight in summer.

conveniently making use of the piste weaving beneath the cables between pylons 6 and 7, all of which are helpfully numbered. Higher up the piste returns beneath pylons 8 and 9, and here Pic des Quatre Termes, not clearly seen until now, towers above you, to the left. Slightly to the right you can pick out two minor cols separated by a small promontory; the left of these is your objective, though either would suffice, and in fact the ascent to the col on the right is slightly less steep.

The way onwards and upwards begins on a cairned route through a chaos of massive blocks on the left of the piste, and is the most tiring part of the ascent. The southern col is named, Brèche de Contadé, from its proximity to Pic du Contadé, so the more northerly of the two could be called the Brèche Nord de Contadé. From here a fine arête ascends in a northerly direction, and affords some delightful scrambling to a summit with an immense panorama. Walkers not adept at scrambling may descend a little from the col, towards the northeast, and re-ascend by a cairned path to the summit.

Ascent: 3h: Descent: 2h

Walk 89 Pic de Madamète (2657m: 8717ft) Grade B and Vallée d'Aygues-Cluses (2150m: 7054ft) Grade C The granite massif of Néouvielle is renowned for its wealth of lakes and small tarns, and offers walkers numerous days of wandering between valleys. From the north the key to this region is the vallée d'Aygues-Cluses, criss-crossed by a vast network of underground streams, from where its name is derived, and rich in flora and wildlife.

The route described here provides three walks in one: many walkers content themselves with the stretch between the start at the Pont de la Gaubie and the Cabane d'Aygues-Cluses, an excellent outing in itself, and little more than a steady stroll along a section of the GR10. Beyond the Cabane the GR10 continues to the Col de Madamète, the boundary of the Réserve Naturelle de Néouvielle, and this, too, provides an acceptable point from which to return. Stronger walkers will want to continue to the nearby summit, Pic de Madamète, which from the Col demands little more than a short, sharp pull. To make a clockwise circuit, the route can be continued west into the adjoining valley and descended to visit the lakes, Nère and Dets Coubous. This stretch is tiring, and, until the main track through the valley is reached, entirely off footpaths.

In the Vallée d'Aygues-Cluses.

Pic de Madamète (right) and Pic d'Estibère from Lac de Coueyla-Gran.

From Luz-St Sauveur the road to the Col du Tourmalet is a test piece for would-be Tour de France cyclists. It climbs steadily, passing numerous tiny villages perched precariously on hillsides, to Barèges, hemmed in on the north by a long and undulating grassy ridge which culminates in Pic du Midi de Bigorre. About three kilometres beyond Barèges the main valley is joined from the south by the vallée d'Aygues-Cluses, and the road makes an unavoidable detour to maintain its gradual ascent. At its southernmost point you reach the Pont de la Gaubie where there is a café and a rough-made car park. In summer months especially the hillsides are often dappled with the bright canopies of *parapentes* as groups of students at the nearby school take to the air (or not, as the case may be).

The GR10, which begins a short distance beyond the café (signposted 'Dets Coubous'), heads south from the Pont de la Gaubie, and climbs easily to join a rough but motorable road that leaves the Col du Tourmalet road at 1564m. This continues for 1.5 kilometres until you reach a concrete footbridge shortly after which a National Park signboard indicates a choice of routes. High up to the right you can make out the dam of Lac Dets Coubous and a series of zigzag paths descending from it;

this is the route that will be used on the return journey by walkers who continue over Pic de Madamète.

For the moment continue left into the hanging valley of Aygues-Cluses, with the path running along the left bank of a stream and meandering uneventfully into a region of jumbled boulders. Wild raspberries are plentiful here in summer and everywhere is bright with the colours of wild flowers among which the rhododendron (*ferrugineum*) is prominent (and toxic!). Marmots abound in the Néouvielle massif, and it is not uncommon to see family groups pottering about among the rocks oblivious to passers-by, in spite of being reputably shy creatures. The valley proceeds in an unhurried way, small cascades and shallow pools offering a host of excuses to dawdle, as ahead the fine profile of the Pic d'Aygues-Cluses gradually increases. At one point you need to cross the stream at a shallow ford and ascend into a small forest of pine trees. These pines, which have a very short growing season (only three months each year), live for several centuries and are often found even above 2500m. Beyond the pines, and nearing the Cabane d'Aygues-Cluses, you must recross the stream at a dried up lake, and ascend easily to reach the edge of an immense bowl of

Pic d'Estibère from Pic de Madamète.

grassland encircled by a great arc of mountains.

Two hours of walking from the Pont de la Gaubie brings you to this wild amphitheatre. In it stands the Cabane d'Aygues-Cluses, a small unmanned refuge with room (and mattresses) for six people, and close by the Lac de Coueyla-Gran. For many walkers this is sufficient outing in itself, calling only for a leisurely return the way you have come.

To the south, a little obscured by a low grassy ridge, two mountains dominate the skyline. On the left the twin peaks of Nère and d'Estibère, and to the right the Pic de Madamète. By continuing with the GR10 (marked by red and white flashes on the rocks) you rise, a little more energetically, to the Lacs de Madamète, and on eventually to the Col de Madamète. Just below the Col a spill of boulders from Pic d'Estibère calls for care and attention, and then you reach the Col, with an immense view southwards to the mountain frontier with Spain.

From the Col, where there is a National Park information

Nèouvielle from the summit of Pic de Madamète.

board, the ascent to the summit (waymarked by blue izards painted on white squares on the rocks) is not unduly long, and the summit of the mountain, with its grandstand view of the Pic de Néouvielle and its attendant Ramoun, is marked by a large cairn.

The easiest way back to Pont de la Gaubie is to retrace one's outward route, but strong walkers might like to descend northwards (the start of the descent being marked by a small cairn a few metres from the summit) to a broad col, and then northwestwards across a wide field of boulders that can be very trying on weary legs. Your objective is Lac Nère, and the approximate line of descent sketched in blue on the 1:25000 map (1747 ouest). In its lower reaches, near Lac Nère (Noir on the 'Top 25' Néouvielle map), the way is cairned through the boulders, but there is no easy going until you reach the main path through the valley on the other side of the lake, and then you can make good progress to the dam of Lac Dets Coubous.

Cross the dam and continue to a small cabane beyond which a

Looking north to Pic du Midi de Bigorre, from the summit of Pic de Madamète.

path zigzags downwards to meet the outward route into the valley d'Aygues-Cluses at the National Park signpost. An easy descent is then made to Pont de la Gaubie.

Ascent: (Cabane d'Aygues-Cluses) 2h 15: (Col de Madamète) 3h 30: (Pic de Madamète) 4h

Descent: (Cabane d'Aygues-Cluses) 1h 45: (Col de Madamète) 2h 15: (Pic de Madamète by either route) 2h 30

Walk 90 Turon de Néouvielle (3035m: 9957ft) Grade B The Turon de Néouvielle, little more than a kilometre southwest of the Pic de Néouvielle, belongs to the easier regiment of 3000m+ summits in the Pyrenees. Yet its remoteness means that of all the summits in this book, Turon is one where an overnight stay in a refuge (La Glère), or camping, is the only way to avoid an otherwise long day. Fortunately, La Glère is more of an hotel than a mountain refuge, with a full restaurant service, heating and showers, and with 90 places, usually open from the beginning of July to the end of September. Walkers arriving by car may drive to La Glère, by a long and winding road, but there is only limited parking for non-residents at La Glère, and few places along its length to park safely.

This relative inaccessibility typifies many of the peaks in the Néouvielle region, unquestionably for the better. By way of compensation the ascent from La Glère goes a long way to demonstrating why Néouvielle is renowned for its mountain lake scenery.

Access to La Glère: About 2 kilometres (1.25 miles) east of Barèges on the road to the Col du Tourmalet a minor, narrow and less than perfect road doubles back across wooded slopes and then by a long and sinuous route (9 kilometres: c.5 miles) into the valley. From the D918, the route is signposted 'Route du Lienz'. In a few places along this road it is possible to park a car and continue on foot, but this is only advised if it is essential to complete the ascent in one day.

From Barèges (and on foot) a road (signposted, and starting from the upper end of the village) leads to a track which rises in zigzags to extensive woodland crossed by a number of walks and ski pistes. The route to be followed climbs in wide bends, and reaches the Glère valley and its road just after passing a ski jump. Continue now up the road, finishing in zigzags to the Lac de la Glère, from where it is a short distance to the hotel, overlooking the lake. Three hours will be needed from Barèges.

Anyone intending to stay at La Glère should enquire first about vacancies at the Office du Tourisme in Barèges.

Turon de Néouvielle: From La Glère follow the undulating path for the Refuge Packe southwards, leaving this about five minutes after a concrete footbridge where the path forks. Keep left here, passing between the Lac de la Mourèle, below and on the left, and the higher and larger Lac det Mail. Continue to follow the river towards the south, passing a small dyke on the left. The path becomes less obvious now, but the general direction south-southeast remains the same and climbs through the ubiquitous boulderfield to a small lake (2433m), beyond which rises an abrupt rock wall which can be turned easily by a cairned path.

Continue following the cairned path and soon the way becomes more obvious, heading now rather more to the south. Keep the Lacs Verts to the left, and shortly pass a small lake and then Lac Bleu (2651m), known collectively with others as the Lacs de Maniportet. Ascend south, along the top of moraine issuing from what remains of the Glacier de Maniportet, and then clamber over easy rocks to reach the ridge linking the Turon with the Pic des Trois Conseillers at 2998m. A little more easy clambering will bring you in ten minutes to the summit of the Turon, and its splendid panorama.

Ascent: 3h: Descent: 2h

Descending from the Hourquette d'Aubert into pleasant woodland.

An alternative descent may be made through the Coume Estrète, a route for some reason generally not described or recommended, but just as easy as the above line of ascent, and a logical descent that need trouble no one.

Follow the Turon's northwest ridge easily down to the Col de Coume Estrète. The direction is always north, and keeping the two Lacs Estelat (2432m and 2399m), Lac de la Manche and Lac dets Mail always on the right. As the upper corrie is descended so a cairned track will be found, and eventually the

Ramoun and Néouvielle, seen above Lac d'Aubert.

line of ascent described above will be intersected northwest of Lac det Mail.

Descent: 2h 30

The ascent of Turon de Néouvielle is a popular walk by the above route; walkers wanting a little more solitude need only reverse the circuit, ascending first to the Col de Coume Estrète, with the likelihood that many walkers will return by their outward route. The complete circuit however is among the finest walking the Pyrenees have to offer.

Walk 91 Hourquette d'Aubert (2498m: 8195ft) and Pic dets Coubous (2647m: 8684ft) Grade C Like many of the high mountain passes of the Pyrenees, the Hourquette d'Aubert is not without an expansive and impressive panorama. It lies very much at the heart of the Néouvielle Nature Reserve and is a significant link between the vallée de Neste d'Aure to the south and the valleys of Barèges and Bastan to the north. Not surprisingly the walk to this prominent col is a popular outing and without difficulty, especially from the car park beside the lake from which it takes its name.

The great serpentine approach by road from Fabian, near Aragnouet, is quite an experience and brings you by Lac d'Orédon to the edge of Lac d'Aumar, before a descent to the car park. Not immediately obvious from the map is the fact that the height lost in driving down to the car park needs to be regained on foot as you reascend northwards to the northwestern end of Lac d'Aumar. By parking at the side of the road to the east of spot height 2197 overlooking Lac d'Aumar, the GR10, an obvious path may be followed to the far end of the lake without loss of height; it makes life easier on the return journey, too.

The whole walk is framed by the massive mound of Pic de Néouvielle and its acolyte, Ramoun, its great northeastern

Finally approaching the Hourquette d'Aubert, with Lac d'Aubert and Lac d'Aumar beyond.

The view northwards from the Hourquette d'Aubert.

slopes between the Crête de Barris d'Aubert and the Crête d'Espade bare, barren and often retaining snow well into the summer months.

Not far from the inflow to Lac d'Aumar a signpost points out a rising path to Col d'Aubert, climbing easily to the upper edge of Aubert's wooded slopes. The conspicuous summit (three small bumps from this angle) of Pic de Madamète lies to the north (see Walk 89 for an ascent from the vallée d'Aygues-Cluses to the north, though it can be ascended less demandingly from Lac d'Aumar to Col de Madamète).

As the cliffs of Pic dets Coubous assume greater prominence than those of Pic de Madamète you traverse a spill of massive boulders that, were it not for someone's hard effort in constructing a walkway through them, would be excruciatingly difficult. As it is, little effort is required to reach the end of the rising path, conspicuous from afar, that leads more or less directly to the col and a splendid view northwards to Pic d'Astazou, and over Lac Nère (Noir), Lac Blanc and Lac dets Coubous.

Ascent: 1h: Descent: 0h 45

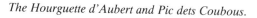

The Hourguette d'Aubert and Pic dets Coubous.

On the summit of Pic de Madamète, looking along the ridge to Pic dets Coubous.

From the hourquette it is an easy uphill plod to the ridge rising rockily to the Pic Dets Coubous.
Ascent: 0h 30: Descent: 0h 30

Walkers not intimidated by drops on either side will experience no difficulty continuing along the crest to Pic de Madamète and its col, for a speedy descent to Lac d'Aumar to conclude a delightful circuit.

Lac d'Aumar.

Walk 92 Tour of Lacs and Vallée d'Aygues-Cluses by Hourquette d'Aubert (2498m: 8195ft) and Col de Madamète (2509m: 8232ft) Grade C This superb circuit may be accomplished as easily from the north (Pont de la Gaubie) as from Lac d'Aubert; the route from the south is slightly shorter. The description given here is a clockwise circuit, and has the advantage of gaining the first col, the Hourquette d'Aubert quite speedily, and with only a short descent to be made towards the end of the walk from Col de Madamète.

Follow Walk 91 to the Hourquette d'Aubert and from there descend northwards in a series of zigzags to pick a way through a charming sequence of lakes, Estagnol, Nére (Noir), Blanc, Dera Yunco and dets Coubous, as well as numerous tiny lakelets. Cross the barrage of Lac dets Coubous and pass around the cabane to descend in sweeping zigzags to the vallée d'Aygues Cluses. Here you meet the GR10 which now heads eastwards into the valley (see Walk 89, though little description is necessary) to the Cabane d'Aygues-Cluses, from where Walk 89 leads to the Col de Madamète before a swift descent to Lac d'Aumar.

Time: 6h

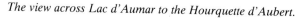

The view across Lac d'Aumar to the Hourquette d'Aubert.

Good signposting is a noticeable feature of most walks in and around the Pyrenean National Park.

Walk 93 Pic de Néouvielle (3091m: 10,141ft) Grade B The Pic de Néouvielle was first climbed in 1847. Countless ascents have followed, for Néouvielle is among the most frequented of Pyrenean summits, which should not be allowed to disguise the fact that the mountain is not an easy ascent, calling for an ice-axe and, towards the end of the season when the remains of

Lac d'Aumar, quiet now, but a popular sunbathing spot at weekends.

snow slopes are hard, crampons, too, could prove welcome. Fortunately, many of the difficulties of this nature can be avoided by a little granitic scrambling.

93a Via the Hourquette d'Aubert Walk 91 should be used to gain the Hourquette d'Aubert from where a path sets off southwest along a narrowing ridge, shortly to pass on to the side overlooking Lac d'Aubert in order to reach a large bouldery hollow. Continue south across the boulderfield and pass beneath the Crête d'Espade to the foot of the obvious Brèche de Chausenque (2790m) to which a line of cairns leads. Ignore this route, and continue southwest over low rock terraces to the Ramoun glacier/snowfield on the northeast side of Néouvielle; each year's weather conditions very much determine how easy or difficult the following section might be, but properly equipped walkers should experience no difficulty. Climb the glacier/snowfield, steeply at first, to its highest point, aiming right of the obvious gap between Ramoun (3014m) and Néouvielle, and leave the glacier following a line of cairns (if they are visible) and an indistinct path across the northeast face to the north-northeast spur. Here a path is encountered,

On the Hourquette d'Aubert. The line of ascent for Néouvielle continues along the ridge, left, for a while.

Ramoun and Néouvielle.

coming from the north. Go left here and scramble over easy rocks to the summit.

The summit panorama is excellent; close by a long shattered ridge runs south to Pic Long, with Mont Perdu (Monte Perdido) beyond. To the southwest rise the Gavarnie peaks, west is Vignemale with Pic d'Anie beyond that. The Pic du Midi de Bigorre is conspicuous to the north, while less obvious, to the east, the view extends as far as Andorra.

Ascent: (From Lac d'Aubert) 3h 30: Descent: 2h 30

93b Via La Brecque de Barris From the Aubert car park head south to cross the dam of the lake, and at its western extremity take a waymarked path going southwest across easy grassy/ rocky slopes. At about 2260m the route curves right (west then north) climbing several rock terraces and easy boulders. Continue on a waymarked route to the Brecque de Barris (2439m), a gap (unnamed on most maps) along the east-northeast arête of Ramoun, beyond which the track descends a little before continuing across the slope, climbing slightly, through a region of large boulders.

Rough going among the boulders above Lac de Cap de Long.

Continue across this vast granite slope heading for the Brèche de Chausenque until the route from the Hourquette d'Aubert is met and followed to the summit. No well trodden line exists; but on such a popular summit it is likely that traces of those who have immediately gone before you will be found in abundance; with caution they may be followed.

Ascent: 3h: Descent: 2h

Walk 94 Lac de Cap de Long (2350m: 7710ft) Grade C and Pic de Campbieil (3173m: 10,410ft) Grade B In a great mountain hollow south of Pic de Néouvielle lies Lac de Cap de Long, its waters reflecting black, blue or jade as the light bounces back and forth from the surrounding peaks. Once this long, curving lake was a place of natural beauty, accompanied to the southeast by a smaller lake, Lac Loustalat, surrounded by pine trees. Then the demands of Electricité de France brought first a raising of the water level by some 30m, effectively doubling the length of the lake, and then by another 130m, which finally saw the drowning of the smaller lake. When Cap de Long is full it is a magnificent sight, and the short walk along its south bank an energetic incursion into the savage arena that lies beyond.

Ascending into the bleak landscape beyond Lac de Cap de Long.

At the western end of the lake the valley swings to the south, known here as the Montagne de Cap Long, at the head of which rises the great bulk of Pic de Campbieil, vying with Le Taillon for the distinction of being the easiest 3000m summit in the Pyrenees, though somewhat less interesting an ascent.

During his second visit to the Pyrenees in 1792 the pioneering explorer and mountaineer Baron Ramond de Carbonnières, constantly found inaccuracies in the maps of the day, and wrote in his journal: 'May Heaven preserve the Pyrenees from an earthquake big enough to make the map correct!' The echoes of that sentiment may still resound within the cloistered corridors of the Institut Géographique National for here, in the back of beyond, they have removed Pic Badet from its rightful place southeast of Pic Long and placed it in a spot hitherto occupied by Pic de Campbieil, and vice versa. Either the maps (IGN 'Top 25' 1748 ET: Néouvielle and 1748 OT: Gavarnie) are wrong, or three sets of French guide books, all by experienced Pyrenean mountaineers. For the purposes of Walk 94, walkers with either of these maps are asked to read 'Pic de Campbieil'

(3173m) for 'Pic Badet' (3160m), and vice versa. So far as can be judged such major errors are unusual on IGN maps, which otherwise may safely be relied upon.

That a visit to Lac de Cap de Long is a popular weekend outing may be evinced from the presence near the barrage of a number of small bar/restaurants that in summer do a roaring trade in beers, *crêpes*, postcards and souvenirs. The car park is not overlarge, but parking continues beyond the bars. One French guidebook mentions that the car park here is subject to 'stonefall'; this is true, indeed many of the 'stones' weigh about 70 tons! To avoid having to remove too many terminally redesigned cars the authorities have placed a limit to the parking area, and beyond this a path weaves in and out of 'stones' to reach the edge of the former lakeside path. Not surprisingly, with rocks constantly dropping from fragile cliffs that even crag martins think twice about nesting on, the old path has been abandoned for a higher, safer but more demanding one that twists and turns upwards to a point where it leaves the Néouvielle Nature Reserve and enters the National Park. More or less horizontal now the path continues southwest, the steep southeastern side of Pic de Néouvielle dropping dramatically into the lake.

Above Lac de Cap de Long.

Pic Méchant from Lac de Cap de Long.

Slowly the view into the valley of Montagne de Cap de Long opens up, as Pic Maubic, Pic Long and (the real) Pic Badet vie for attention. As the path begins to descend to the head of Lac de Cap de Long a retreat should be made by walkers not wishing to continue to Pic de Campbieil.
Time: 1h 45

Ramoun, Néouvielle, Pic des Trois Conseillers across Lac de Cap de Long.

To continue to Pic de Campbieil keep up the valley, past the moraine below Pic Maubic, to a steep rock face which can be climbed easily enough by a route intermittently waymarked, but demanding attention at all times. Higher up the valley climb westwards by a steep grassy couloir to gain the edge of a large boulderfield. Continue south then southeast to pass a small lake (2591m) and gradually upwards, through boulders or on snow slopes according to conditions and the time of year, to another lake, the Gourg de Cap de Long, which remains frozen well into the year. From the lake a direct ascent by a couloir may be made to the principal summit, though less demanding is an ascent to the Hourquette de Cap de Long. From here climb east to ascend unstable boulders steeply to 3157m, then northeast along the left side of the main ridge to the summit.
Ascent: 3h 30: Descent: 2h 30

Walk 95 Pic Long (3192m: 10,472ft) Grade A Although the highest Pyrenean mountain wholly in France, Pic Long receives far fewer visits than its neighbour, Pic de Néouvielle. The comparative ease of access accounts for some of Néouvielle's attention, while Pic Long demands an approach

Lac de Cap de Long.

along the south side of Lac de Cap de Long, no straightforward undertaking in itself, followed by a good measure of uphill walking, off trail, through boulderfields, across glaciers and snowfields, and the ascent of a rock chimney . . . no place for a Sunday picnic! In essence, Pic Long is very much the preserve of experienced mountaineers and regular, fit walkers, accustomed if need be to using ice-axe, crampons and a rope.

The idiosyncrasies of the approach along the south side of Lac de Cap de Long are detailed in Walk 94, and are generally sufficient to deter less than committed curiosity. Continuing along this path the broad valley south of the lakehead, which shares with the surrounding mountains the collective name, Montagne de Cap de Long, is gained (near the convergence of two streams at about 2300m) by a slightly descending and then rising traverse: Pic de Campbieil is the conspicuous summit at the head of the valley.

Ascend on the true left (west) bank of the stream convergence, following a line of cairns marking the route over rock terraces and around boulders, steep enough in places to demand the use of hands. The path edges to the right as it climbs in order to pass around a hillock (2591m) beyond which a small lake will be found. Keep the lake on the left and climb south-southwest into a cwm from which issues the stream of Cap de Long, always in the general direction of the pyramidal Pic Badet.

Gradually you reach the foot (2786m) of a long lateral moraine running east into the valley from Pic Maubic, an outlier of Pic Long. The moraine issues from the glacier east of Pic Long, the Glacier de Pays Baché. Turn the end of the moraine and ascend snow slopes towards the glacier; if the snow is firm, now is the time to put crampons on, in any event they will almost certainly be needed on the glacier. It is also worth considering whether to use a rope for the added security of the party.

Above and a little to the left of the summit cone a small notch appears on the ridge. This is the Hourquette du Pic Long (3099m) to which all tracks across the snowfield and glacier now converge, and it is the lowest point of the crest linking Pic Long and Pic Badet. Ascend the glacier heading towards the Hourquette, finishing steeply on snow from which the entry into the ensuing chimney can be awkward, depending on the height of snow against the rock. The chimney, which must now be climbed, is steep (about 30m), but not otherwise difficult, and places you on the Hourquette.

Start ascending the ridge towards Pic Long, but after a few minutes traverse left on to a ledge leading on to the south face until more or less below the summit, from where a steep but fairly easy gully (some risk of stonefall) leads to the summit. Ascent: 4h: Descent: 3h 30

Walk 96 Lac and Vallée de Badet (2084m: 6837ft) Grade C
Though undoubtedly well known to winter skiers, the flower-decked meadowland of the vallon de Badet is relatively quiet during summer. For this, botanists will be grateful, for the whole valley is a vast carpet of alpine flowers.

The walk begins from the ski village of Piau-Engaly, reached by an inordinately long series of zigzags from Le Plan with its unique belltower and Chapel of the Templars. As Piau-Englay is approached the roadside sprouts a range of car parking signs and instructions that have little significance in summer. Continue ascending the village roads and follow the sign for the 'Quartier de Badet'; this brings you to a large car park, overlooking a two-tier car park, overlooking the valley.

A broad path descends from the parking place, nursery ski slope on the left, to the Télésiège de Mouscadès, from where the path (a piste in fact) sets off up the valley. Shortly, a path descends on the right (signposted 'Port de Campbieil') to a

Lac de Badet.

The great sweep of the Crête des Cintes Blanques (Badet valley).

footbridge (Walk 97). Ignore this and continue further along the piste until a side track drops to a bridge across the stream; a hidden cabin stands nearby.

At this point you can either cross the stream, or follow the prominent path on the right bank, which for a time takes a more direct line to Lac de Badet. The left bank, that is, the valley bottom, is the one to take if it is flowers you are in search of.

The slopes on the south side of the valley are the reserve of skiers, while the soaring ridges that climb to the north and west to the summits of Pic Méchant, the Crête des Cintes Blanques, and the Pics d'Estaragne look quite impregnable, which for the most part they are. The variety of colour in the different rock strata is another fascinating aspect of this remarkable valley.

From the footbridge, the next two kilometres are a botanists paradise, the walking easy as a shallow series of cascades and then more prominent waterfalls come and go. Finally, a little uphill work is needed to reach a bridge crossing the stream that drains this upper valley basin. Beyond this a small shelter, the Refuge de Badet, provides basic accommodation in an emergency. The lake itself is small, and nestles at the foot of a steep slope rising to Pic du Piau. (As late as August, there can still be snow around the edge of the lake and high in the mountain corries.)

You can return the way you came, or by descending above the right bank of the Neste de Badet. If so, do not recross the upper footbridge, but follow a path (signposted 'Piau') that descends gradually and provides a fine view of the more impressive waterfalls en route. This path eventually joins the upper end of the piste along which the walk began, and by means of which an easy finish may be made.

Ascent: 1h 30: Descent: 1h (no allowance for flower spotting!)

Walk 97 Port de Campbieil (2596m: 8517ft) Grade B, and Soum des Salettes (2976m: 9764ft) Grade B The Port de Campbieil is the link between the curving valley of the Neste de Badet and that of Campbieil, a long sinuous valley that reaches the main valley, the Gave de Pau, near Gèdre. It is perfectly feasible to reach the Port de Campbieil from Gèdre, but an alternative approach from the east, via the vallée de Badet with its myriad species of alpine flowers, has much to commend it.

The walk, like Walk 96, begins at the ski resort of Piau-Engaly; indeed both walks share the same valley, but at different altitudes, and therefore with vastly differing perspectives. The initial descent, west, from the car park in the Quartier de Badet soon leads to a path (signposted 'Port de Campbieil') descending, right, to a footbridge across the valley river. The path continues, climbing easily westwards to the shepherds' Cabane de Moune, and then with more sense of purpose upwards to gain a broad platform running south with the valley's axis.

In the upper reaches of the Badet valley.

A quiet approach along this section may well reveal izards or some of the marmot colony in the many burrows and crevices along the way. Spare a moment, too, to take in the variegated rock strata, yellow-orange and purple, notably of Pic Méchant, the Crête des Cintes Blanques, and the Pics d'Estaragne, that stand out conspicuously from the otherwise grey cliff faces and chough-loud pinnacles.

The platform, a kind of elongated balcony from which to view the valley and its peaks, rises steadily, until it meets a short rise, tackled in zigzags, and leading to a junction with a path continuing southwards to the HRP. The route now heads steeply northwest, across boulder slopes, and in a long series of tiring zigzags to the Port de Campbieil, where a prolonged rest would be in order. Immediately to the north is the isolated summit, Lenquo de Capo (2716m: 8911ft), and to the south, rather more distant, the Soum des Salettes. The view down the

River detail in the Badet valley.

In the Badet valley. The Port de Campbieil lies just above the patch of snow to the left of the pointed summit, Lenquo de Capo.

Campbieil valley is quite impressive, but by continuing a short distance to the right, a better view opens up of the Cirque de Troumouse in particular.
Ascent: 2h 30: Descent: 1h 45

Walkers continuing to the Soum des Salettes for the spectacular view of the cirques of Troumouse, Estaubé and Gavarnie, will manage its easy northern slopes of rock and grass in little more than an hour, with the same time required for descent.

Walk 98 Lac de l'Oule (1830m: 6003ft) Grade D A modest, yet satisfying outing awaits walkers undertaking the complete circuit of the Lac de l'Oule. All the effort, such as it is, lies in the climb to the lake, while the walk around it is virtually flat. Near the dam there is a refuge, built by the Commune de Saint Lary, and this often serves refreshments, as well as providing accommodation (about 30 places) for walkers setting off for higher pastures.

The ascent begins from a parking area (1591m) along the road to Lac d'Orédon, just above the Cascade de Letz and about one kilometre beyond the first significant hairpin bends. The nearby river, the Neste de Couplan, is crossed by a bridge beyond which a broad, graded track begins a wide sweep, gaining height easily, above the valley, which soon starts to fall away steeply on the right.

After one kilometre the track starts a series of zigzags that lead without much effort to the dam of the lake; the refuge lies across the dam wall, which provides suitable nest sites for crag martins. The lake itself is entirely artificial and serves a factory at Eget. In an agreeable setting, it is hemmed in by wooded slopes on the west and north and by bare hillside rising steeply on the east.

The tour of the lake is equally pleasant in either direction. At the far end of the lake, against a backdrop of wooded slopes and towering peaks, stands a small shelter, the Cabane de la Lude, used as a refuse disposal point by campers.

Time: (Lac de l'Oule and return only) 2h: (Lac de l'Oule and tour of the lake) 3h-3h 30

Walk 99 Lac de Port Bielh (Lac de Bastan)(2285m: 7497ft)
Grade C The lakes contained by the long Crête de Port-Bielh, Pic de Bastan and Pic d'Aygues-Cluses lie in a wild hollow, grey, sombre and impressive.

Walk 98 leads you as far as the Cabane de la Lude at the

Lac de l'Oule marks the start of a number of popular excursions into the Néouvielle Reserve.

northern end of Lac de l'Oule from where the GR10 sets off up the hillside. Follow this only for a few metres, enough to leave behind the broad track around Lac de l'Oule, and then seek out a less than obvious path, initially wet, heading north into woodland. Once located there is no doubt about the route as it meanders through a forest of pines that have seen better times, many of them collapsed and looking much as though a hurricane has just passed through.

The trail through the forest seems to go on for an eternity, with Pic de Bastan looming gradually larger ahead, but seeming to come no nearer. Eventually, as you break clear of the trees a corrugated iron cabane is encountered close by Lac Vert (not named on most maps), beyond which the path climbs to the Laquets de Port-Bielh (2203m). The path squeezes between two of the lakes and continues along the right bank of the stream issuing from Lac de Port-Bielh, later crossing the stream as the Refuge de Port-Bielh and its lake are finally approached, against a stern backdrop of craggy, boulder-strewn slopes. Looking backwards, there is a splendid view down the vallon de l'Oule.

Ascent: 3h: Descent: 2h 30

Walk 100 Soum de Matte (2377m: 7799ft) Grade C One of the most conspicuous features from the town of St Lary is the Téléphérique du Pla d'Adet, much used in winter by skiers and in summer by the local *parapente* training school. Apart from the *téléphérique*, the metalwork of the popular ski resort of Le Pla d'Adet is unsuspected from the valley, for it is gained only by a long, yet immensely attractive, drive through the villages of Vignec and Soulan (whose street lights seem to hang like Christmas decorations on the darkened mountainside). Here, high along the flanks of the Espiaube valley, lie the resorts of Le Cabane and Le Pla d'Adet, forlorn and half dead places in summer.

The beauty of Soum de Matte lies not in its ease of ascent, in fact it has three distinct 'ups' to test the legs of anyone, but in its breathtaking panorama, restricted only to the west by the higher Pic d'Arrouye.

From Le Pla d'Adet (parking just about anywhere in summer) puzzle a way through the streets heading in the direction of the prominent dome, not the Soum de Matte, but the Baby de Soum. Soon however a lower, more shapely summit appears, to which a fine ridge ascends. This is the crest of the Montagne d'Auria, and a fine energetic introduction to the walk. In spite of the apparently steep ascent required (more apparent than real) the climb up the ridge is exhilarating, attention held all the time by the fine array of peaks to the south, prominent among which is the Pic d'Aret with its high-mountain river valley rising above the afforested lower slopes. An easy path picks its way up the crest, while sufferers from vertigo will find an easier and lower path along the northern flank to the col west of the summit, from where an easy stroll leads to the top.

The Baby de Soum awaits, day-trippers making the ascent

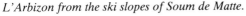

L'Arbizon from the ski slopes of Soum de Matte.

Pic d'Aret from the ascent of Soum de Matte.

*Pic d'Arrouye from the summit of Soum de Matte. The
continuation follows the ridge on the left and climbs steeply to
the summit.*

the easy way by *télésiège*; while 'baby' may have a neatly rounded posterior, its ascent is the steepest part of the walk.

Not far from the *téléski* terminal a large hand-painted topograph is located near the edge of the drop to the Neste d'Aure; now at last all that confusing array of peaks and ridges can be sorted out. To the north the most obvious summit is L'Arbizon, with the less obvious Pic de Monfaucon to its left. But it is the immense view west, south and east that thrills, from the distant cone of Pic de la Munia along the Cirque de Troumouse, across Garlitz and the Pic d'Aret, to the frown of Batoua and Lustou. Far away the mountains run on, for ever it seems, until you finally convince yourself you can see the Med, while to the northeast, could that distant frieze of white really be the Alps?

A steady haul now leads to the terminal of the Téléski de Soum de Matte, generally not in service during summer, and beyond it a final steep pull, disconcerting in one of two places, though nowhere dangerous, to a narrow and neat summit.
Ascent: 2h 30: Descent: 2h

Pic de Garlitz and the Cirque de Troumouse from the northeast. Pic de la Munia is the pointed peak right of centre skyine.

From the col below Baby de Soum a more direct return may be made to Le Pla d'Adet by using the piste that parallels the Téléski de la Ludette.

Back on the summit of Soum de Matte, the tower of Pic d'Arrouye (2566m: 8419ft) lies ahead, reached by a narrow arête and steep climb (Grade B), its summit finally opening up the view to the west, across the vast Néouvielle massif and the shimmering purple hollows that contain Lac de Cap de Long, Lac d'Aubert and Lac d'Aumar. To reach it will extend the walk by one hour in each direction, but it is an extension best left to walkers experienced on friable rock and steep grassy gullies.

USEFUL ADDRESSES AND ORGANISATIONS

Amis du Parc National des Pyrénées, 32, rue Samonzet, 64000 PAU Tel: 59 27 15 30

'Friends of the National Park', organising excursions into the mountains, particularly to study flowers, geology, mountain ways of life, and skiing.

Bureau des Guides, Maison de la Montagne, 65120 LUZ-ST SAUVEUR Tel: 62 92 87 28

Provides courses of instruction in rock and snow climbing, mountain excursions to all major peaks, and a weekly programme of walks between 15 June and 15 September.

CIMES Pyrénées (Centre Information Montagnes et Sentiers), BP742, 65007 TARBES Tel: 62 93 57 57

Information centre about the whole range and both sides of the Pyrenees, including accommodation (gîtes d'étape), routes, general advice, programmes of walks, and 'Randonnées en Kit' (ie 5-7 day walks completely arranged by CIMES, including accommodation and food, etc. but not supervised).

Parc National des Pyrénées, 59, route de Pau, 65000 TARBES Tel: 62 93 30 60

Concerned with the planning and management of the national park; also offers numerous services to walkers, including guided walks and mountain hostels.

Randonnées Pyrénéennes, 29, rue Marcel-Lamarque, 65000 TARBES Tel: 62 93 66 03

Publication and distribution of topoguides, books and maps about the Pyrenees.

SOME PYRENEAN TERMS

There are a number of dialects in regular use on both sides of the Pyrenees, and many colloquial words and expressions have found their way on to maps. The following summary, which is by no means exhaustive, may help walkers glean some idea of the features to be found in regions they intend to enter.

araillous, arralhos	rocky, stony
arou, aroun, aredoun, arredon, redon	round
arres	cracked or fissured limestone rocks
arrouy, rouyo, royo	red
arriu, arriou	stream, brook
artigue	pasturage created by clearance
arribet	small stream
aygue, aigue, ague	water
ayous	billberries
baradat	enclosed place
bal, bat, batch, baight, vath	valley
barranc, barranco	ravine
bassia	a place for gathering sheep
bieilh, vielh	old
blanque, blanca	white
borde	barn or sheepfold
boum	small, deep lake
brèque, brèca	gap, break
caillaou, calhaù	isolated rock
caillaouas	rubble
campana	bell or pointed rock
capera, caperan	pointed rock ie 'gendarme'
canau, canaou	steep gully
cap	prominent summit

castet	fortified hillock
courade, corada	col or through route
courtau, courtaou, cuyeou, coueyla, cujala, coral, courau	shieling, or a place where cattle or sheep are gathered during summer months
crabe	goat
culaous, culaus	a hollow, or cavity
embarraten	closed
estibe	summer pasturage in the mountains
espade, espada	sword
espugne, espalungue, espelunga	grotto
estan, estany, estanio	lake
facha, faja	cornice through which a route or path passes
fag, fach, faig, faigt	beech tree
forat, fourat	a hole, a cave or chasm
forc, fourc, fourcat	forked
gave	mountain river
gourg, gourga	deep lake
labasse, lauze, lause	a wide, flat 'stone' ie rock slab
laquette, laqueta	small lake
louseras	a slaty region
mailh, mail	isolated rock
marcadau	(literally) a market place, but also a walking region
mourène	brown
major, mayou	major, principal
néou	snow
nère, né	black
neste	mountain river
oueillère, houeillassat	words associated with ewes
orri, orry	dry stone cabin

oule, oulette, oulète	a hollow, or mountain cirque
pale	steep, grassy slope
paloume, paloma	wood pigeon
pas, passe	a narrow passage/through route
pne	a long, flat summit
peyre	isolated rock or boulder
pla, plan	stretch of flat ground
port, porteille, pourtère	frontier col
pourtet, portalet, pourtalet	small col, passage
prat, pradère	meadow
pujol, puyo, pouey, pouy	a rise, or a hill
punta	point, summit
quebe, quieba, cova	shelter beneath rocks
raillère, arralhère	scree slope
rio, riu, rieu, riou	watercourse
sède, sèda	a seat, or some prominent feature
seilh	glacier
senda, sender	footpath
serre, serrat	long crest
soula, soulane	(literally) the sunny side of a mountain eg south face
soum	round summit
tort	winding
toue	shelter beneath rocks
tourrat, torrat	frozen
tramezaygues	region between two watercourses
tuc, tusse, tuque	secondary summit